MATCHING
PASTORAL
CANDIDATES
AND
CHURCHES

MATCHING PASTORAL CANDIDATES AND CHURCHES

A Guide for Search Committees and Candidates

Joseph Umidi

Matching Pastoral Candidates and Churches: A Guide for Search Committees and Candidates

Published by Kregel Ministry, an imprint of Kregel Publications, 2450 Oak Industrial Dr. NE, Grand Rapids, MI 49505.

Formerly *Confirming the Pastoral Call*

Library of Congress Cataloging-in-Publication Data
Umidi, Joseph L.
  Confirming the pastoral call: a guide to matching candidates and congregations / by Joseph L. Umidi.
  p.   cm.
Includes bibliographical references.
  1. Pastoral search committees. 2. Clergy—Appointment, call, election. I. Title.
BV664 U65   2000   254 21—dc21   99-043119

ISBN 978-0-8254-4680-1

Printed in the United States of America

1 2 3 4 5 / 27 26 25 24 23 22 21 20

2020-08

CONTENTS

THE WHIRLWIND ROMANCE

Six months after resigning from his church of sixty-five members, Pastor Steve found himself in a difficult financial bind: emergency funds were dried up and so was his part-time water-filter business. His wife also had just given birth to their sixth child. After months of praying and searching for another pastoral call, he finally saw some light on the horizon. It came in the form of a small country church that almost overnight had grown in attendance from eighty to 320. With little warning, the pastor had resigned to take a megachurch in another city. Now down to 120, and losing members by the week, the little church anxiously asked Steve to come and preach. He was elated. It seemed to be the perfect solution, and just in time.

The next Sunday, Steve preached both morning and evening services under a powerful anointing. Touched by God, several church members came to the altar; others couldn't help remarking on the strong presence of the Lord they felt. The chairman of the elder board said, "I haven't seen God move like this in years." Later that evening, while Steve was preparing his family for the two-hundred-mile drive home, a hastily convened meeting resulted in the board unanimously extending Steve a call, right there on the spot.

The next day, Steve walked into my office energized, his emotions swirling. After gently bringing him back down to earth, I said something that hit him like a bucket of ice water on a hot summer beach: "Steve, long-term relationships aren't built on infatuation. They are built on the bonding of common values. The anointing on your message doesn't guarantee that you and the church will have the same mission. God's gifts, either yours or the church's, are no guarantee of God's confirmation. It takes patience and character on the part of both the pastoral candidate *and* the search committee to wait for God to confirm a call."

Because of our relationship, Steve knew I was not minimizing the importance of the "connection" between the potential pastor and the congregation by a movement of the Holy Spirit. Church groups that prioritize "anointing" in the preaching and ministry of their pastors look for this "connection" with a candidate. However, our research has revealed that churches that rely heavily on the role of the "anointed message" in the confirmation process do not gain a statistical advantage in the longevity of their new staff over those who emphasize different priorities.[1] In too many cases the process itself is flawed and results in weighing only one or two items too heavily. I proposed to Steve, and now to the readers of this book, "a more excellent way."

For the next two hours, I shared with Steve the same guidelines presented in this book. In all my years of personal ministry experience, I have seen repeatedly how a lack of depth in the "courtship" process leading up to the calling of a pastor to a church results in short-term pastorates that cannot withstand the tests of conflict and stress. Although other authors have touched on some of the elements of a successful pastoral candidate evaluation and preparation method, I have never seen a compilation in one volume of the innovative steps contained in the following chapters.

Part 1 helps churches and pastors prepare for a successful match through relationship renewal. Part 2 is written from the perspective of the church that is looking for a new leader, and part 3 is written for the benefit of the pastoral candidate. Regardless of which side of the procedure you are on, you should read all sections in order to understand your own role and to see the process from the other side's perspective.

Just as marital disillusionment often is connected to poor premarital preparation, disillusionment and burnout among church leaders stems from poor or—worse yet—nonexistent candidating procedures. Perfect marriages don't exist, whether between husband and wife or pastor and church, but a well-considered and carefully followed procedure for selecting new leaders (or for a pastoral candidate choosing a new church) can increase the likelihood of creating lasting, vital covenants between churches and their new pastors and staff.

Some would say that simply promoting from within the organization, rather than seeking an "unknown quantity" from the outside, will eliminate the need to deal with the issues in this book. Unfortunately, the evidence shows that even someone promoted from within can turn out to be a serious mismatch. An associate pastor, for example, who might be well-liked and respected in his present role, may not make a suitable senior pastor in the same organization. Any time a leader changes roles, his compatibility with the new office should be carefully and thoroughly evaluated. Power and position are known to corrupt. The only safeguard is to confirm the call in a leader's life and determine how clearly that call matches the needs of the organization and the specific requirements of the position.

From the perspective of the pastoral candidate, an honest look at how your experience, personality, abilities, and expectations fit a particular organization and role is the most fundamental step you can take to protect yourself and your family from being "eaten alive." Stated in a more positive way, a deliberate and thoughtful consideration of your "fit" within an organization and position increases your chances of finding a church where your gifts and vision can soar.

Even with all the books and articles that have been written about the necessity of a "divine call" to the ministry, far too many candidates still enter the pastoral vocation without it. Some enter presumptuously, others with innocent or noble-sounding motives; but without a call from God, there is no way to withstand the pressures that come with advancing the kingdom. We cannot "call" ourselves, and others cannot call us to the ministry. Only God can issue the authentic call that is confirmed by others and evidenced in the fruit of our own fulfillment and sense of destiny.

This is not a book on knowing God's will. It is a book on confirming God's will, especially as it relates to the critical match between churches and their potential leaders.

If you've waited until you need to call a new pastor before you've picked up this book, or if you are a pastor in search of a new position, here's a "red flag" warning: You must back away from the immediacy of your need and look objectively at the process. You will be tempted to rush or shortcut the steps, but if you do, the results could be disastrous.

Remember, you're not merely filling a slot on your staff or looking for a job as a pastor, you're trying to confirm the specific direction of God's call. Confirming the call takes time, patience, and care. Along with God's known ways of revealing His will, this book is a key resource for developing better relationships between churches and their leaders. By the grace of God, we can minimize turnover within the pastorate and maximize joyful "partnerships in the gospel" as we come into the greatest harvest in the history of the church.

PART ONE

A TIME FOR RELATIONSHIP RENEWAL

CHAPTER 1

MATCHES NOT
MADE IN HEAVEN

J ohn was one of our best students. He already had a dozen years of
  pastoral experience before he came to seminary to complete his degree. The other students seemed to gravitate toward him, especially after
they heard him preach in homiletics class. After graduation, he accepted
a call to a growing church in Georgia. This church was a pastor's dream
come true: an influential radio ministry, a thriving Christian day school,
large and sophisticated facilities. We were all certain that John was about
to step into the fullness of his career. After all, he was one of our best
graduates.

One year later, I got the all-too-familiar phone call:

> I'm quitting the ministry. This church isn't what I thought
> it was when I agreed to be its pastor. My wife and I just
> can't take the pressure anymore—we're tired of serv-
> ing people who only want to be served. Can you recom-
> mend me to a teaching position somewhere?

Twenty years ago, sociologist John Norval of Notre Dame claimed that
one in four Catholic priests and one in eight Protestant ministers quit the
ministry each year.[1] More recent estimates suggest that the number of
Protestant ministers who quit each year has grown to one in six, which

12

equates to more than fifty thousand of the nation's total of three hundred fifty thousand ministers. If these numbers are accurate, more pastors quit the ministry each year than attended the historic 1996 Promise Keepers pastor's conference in Atlanta. Imagine each of those forty thousand leaders deciding to leave the ministry on the same day and then emptying the Georgia Dome en masse, and you can begin to see the enormity of this critical situation. Sadly, some of our most able pastors, like John, have joined this massive exodus from the clergy.

What about those who stay in the ministry? Research shows that the most effective and enriching church ministries are those that are led by pastors who have invested at least six years in the same church community.

Church researcher George Barna notes an alarming trend over the past twenty years: The average tenure in the same church for senior pastors has decreased from seven years to four years.[2] Worse yet, Barna reports that six out of every ten senior pastors surveyed say that what they have experienced at their present church has not increased their passion for ministry. When our leaders are not growing in spiritual passion, is it any wonder that the fire of God is lost in the lives of the people?

Clearly, many church leaders, though faithful to their calling, are disillusioned with the ministries they were once certain would bring them many fruitful years of service. A significant part of this crisis stems from an incomplete and often haphazard approach to matching a church's needs with a pastoral candidate's strengths and calling. The resulting disillusionment on both sides, from unfulfilled expectations, has become an unbearable source of stress on pastors and churches in every city and town in America. This book is designed to help churches and potential leaders avoid the painful experience of "mismatching."

Toxic Churches: The Terminators

Many churches today are being inundated by dozens of eager, freshly ordained young men and women applying for limited positions. I interviewed a pastoral candidate in November 1996, who told me that three months prior he had been one of 380 applicants to a particular church in Pennsylvania. While the laborers may be few, the leaders are standing in long lines waiting for doors to open. Unfortunately, what they find once they walk through the open doors may not be what they expected.

It's no secret that far too many churches and Christian ministries have earned horrendous reputations for unfairly terminating staff members or—worse yet—inflicting upon them painful pressure to resign. John C.

LaRue Jr., former research director for *Christianity Today*, revealed that up to one-third of the churches he studied that were conducting a pastoral search had forced the previous pastor to leave, and up to one-fourth of all current pastors have been forced out at some point in their careers.[3] Unfortunately, four out of every ten who were forced out have not yet returned to pastoral ministry.

The shocking part of this phenomenon is that 62 percent of the ousted pastors were forced out by churches that had already done this to one or more pastors in the past. These "repeat offender" churches comprise at least 15 percent of all U.S. churches! They have contributed to the development of a "victim" mentality among a significant number of wounded leaders and their families.

Although a majority of the pastors in the survey were terminated for biblically sound reasons, such as moral or financial compromise, a significant minority (43 percent) were forced out by conflict with a small but influential faction within the congregation, or by one or two members of the church's governing board. According to LaRue, it typically took only seven to ten people (which equated to a mere three or four percent of the congregation) to push the pastor out the door. A significant number of leaders were fired simply because their style conflicted with some small power clique. The majority of these pastors felt that the church's leaders had been deliberately dishonest during the interview process about the history of such conflict patterns within the church.

Pastor Bill sat in the back of our church one Sunday. After the service, he shared with us that he had recently been terminated in a coup led by a small group of leaders who were all family related. After he was fired, he discovered that this church had followed the same course with three other pastors over the years. Bill is now in a national restoration ministry called Pastor in Residence, which mentors wounded leaders back to full confidence in their calling.[4] A good pastor is a terrible thing to waste. We cannot afford to lose even one.

Unlike Pastor Bill, who is on the way toward healing, many terminated pastors carry their pain and disillusionment with them to the next position or to a vocation outside the ordained ministry. Here is what one of them said to us about his termination:

> I felt stunned by what they did and how they did it. . . .
> [I was] told at the church door after the service that I
> was through and not to come back. I felt such a sense of

sadness for Christ's church that a congregation would
be willing to act in such a heartless way; even secular
businesses do not treat their leaders with such contempt.
My emotions felt like they had been dumped on a pile
of scrap metal called shame. I knew that I would be the
subject of discussion down at the local donut shop that
week. After I ran out of "what do I do now, Lord?" cries,
I found that my ability to trust in others had been shattered. I even had a difficult time entrusting myself to
my wife. I felt like a failure as a provider to my family
and an embarrassment to my boys. They were forming
their ideas of what a "man" is by watching how these
people treated their father and how I was responding. . . .
And then came the loneliness. Former associates and
friends distanced themselves from me because "he's in
trouble," "he's involved in something," "where there's
smoke there's fire." What I needed was their love, their
trust, their support. . . . I have personally witnessed abandonment in combat in Southeast Asia and I clearly re-
call the aloneness of the troops who had been isolated
through no action of their own. The same could be said
for pastors who've been squeezed out. Believe me, the
abandonment is one and the same.

What about their families? Think of the upheaval at home when a
spouse is pressured to leave a ministry. LaRue discovered that three-
fourths of these terminated pastoral families had to move out of the area,
and two-thirds of the pastor's spouses had to change jobs. One in ten of
these pastors experienced a major illness within twelve months of being
forced out.

But it is not only the banished pastor and his family who suffer. Toxic
churches also pay a price. Almost ten percent of the congregation will
leave a church that forces a pastoral departure, many of them following
the terminated pastor to his new position.[5]

Toxic Pastors: Conditional Lovers

Because toxic relationships between pastors and churches are often
caused by the pastor himself, today's generation of churchgoers have
learned to question authority. They ask some tough but legitimate

questions, like whether a pastor's faith and commitment is nurturing his own "wholeness." In other words, does the pastor "walk his talk"? Is the pastor's physical, emotional, mental, and spiritual life integrated and healthy, or is he as fragmented as some discredited secular leaders who have crashed and burned in our culture? Leaders who lack balance or wholeness often have a hard time receiving and giving God's unconditional love and grace. The people in the pews begin to wonder whether the gospel being preached will really work for them when it doesn't seem to work for the pastor himself.

"Physician, heal thyself" is the cry of churches whose leaders have self-defeating personality traits; physically destructive lifestyles; addictions to drivenness or other neurotic patterns; or a leadership style rooted in unhealed insecurity, anxiety, or control issues.[6] Too often, a toxic minister finds faults in his parishioners that he is not owning up to in his own life. In Matthew 7:3, Jesus talked about this "splinter and beam" syndrome: "And why do you look at the speck in your brother's eye, but do not consider the plank in your own eye?" (NKJV). Of course, this admonition cuts both ways.

What do churches that terminate toxic pastors cite as the reasons for choosing this painful path? Regrettably, one of the top reasons for a congregation firing a minister is the feeling that they are unliked or conditionally loved by him.[7] The most common expression of conditional love by a minister is his inability to accept parishioners as they are and where they are.

A second reason that churches become disillusioned with their pastors is when they continually hammer home a "pet doctrine," or get stuck on a single emphasis, or preach around their own particular blind spots. This malady has sometimes been called the "hobbyhorse" syndrome, because some pastors get on a particular theme and can't seem to get off. Vocational ministry is a potential breeding ground for a subtle form of idolatry, particularly theological or doctrinal idolatry. Some unbalanced ministers worship their theology of God rather than God Himself.

A third reason for disillusionment is the unexpressed expectations that go with the job. Louis McBurney's list of unrealistic expectations of the average pastor are: He must be sinless, he must be constantly available, he must be capable of meeting any need, he must have no spiritual needs or emotional problems himself, and he must never let on that he has a material need.[8]

Pastors also have unrealistic expectations. One is for them to assume their parishioners will respect them simply because they have the title or office of pastor. Without earning credibility through the way they exercise their authority, these leaders are relying on the limited authority of position rather than the long-term authority of relationship. Ultimately, this will prove as destructive as the man who continually demands his wife submit to him because he has the position of husband, while ignoring his responsibility to love her as Christ loved the church.

Most people simply want to know that their leaders can be trusted and that they know where they are going. Building trust and sharing the vision must be addressed clearly in the "courtship season" before a leader is called. By following the guidelines in this text, churches and candidates can greatly minimize the chances of relational "divorce."

CHAPTER 2

LEAVING AND CLEAVING

The first step in a successful leadership transition is the development of an effective strategy for dealing with the past. Saying farewell to the departing leader and his or her family, accomplishing good closure, and praying for the blessing of a commission in a corporate prayer time is important to your church members and the departing leader. Well-managed closure prepares the congregation for beginning the new courtship process and helps them to remain open to receiving and accepting the unique ministry of a new leader.

The need for a church family to leave behind their bond to a former pastor and freely "cleave" to the new pastor is similar to the prerequisite for marriage given in Genesis 2:24. Authors Gary Smalley and John Trent emphasize that it is more difficult in a new marriage to reach out and form bonds of intimacy and partnership when a husband or wife is still reaching back to the family of origin, hoping to receive a withheld blessing from a parent.[1] In the context of a church and its leaders, it is difficult for a congregation to bond with a new pastor if they are still looking back for closure or a blessing from, in this case, a spiritual father.

Twenty percent of the respondents in our research said that the biggest problems they faced in transitioning to their new positions were the unresolved issues some of the congregation had with the former pastor.

What to Do When the Pastor Unexpectedly Resigns

How a departing leader leaves a church sets the stage for how easily a new leader will become established. Roy Oswald of the Alban Institute notes that "usually they slip off into the night without really saying good-bye, and that can undercut everything they've done up till then. People may question whether the pastor really cared for them at all."[2] As one congregant recalls,

> It all seemed to happen so suddenly. Pastor Jack had rallied us to a new awareness of supporting missions, and we collected our first faith-promise missions offering for the coming year. The final service erupted in victory and praise when we realized that we had gone over our goal! It was a time of great celebration—that is, until Pastor Jack stepped to the pulpit for the benediction. In those next few moments, everything came to a screeching halt. Our pastor told us that God had called him elsewhere, and he would be leaving at the end of the month. And then he slipped out the back door.

Church leaders can help themselves and their members move forward in a positive frame of mind by planning and scheduling an "exit interview" with the resigning pastor or staff leader, followed by an opportunity for the congregation to say farewell. The departing leader will be honored when the remaining leaders show a desire to receive his or her accumulated wisdom and insight as a gift to the church family.

Conducting a Successful Exit Interview

The exit interview should include the elders, pastoral staff, and members of the new search committee. Begin with praise and prayer. As the Lord's presence becomes evident, Scriptures that edify and encourage should be read. Several leaders should then share a few words of sincere appreciation for the departing pastor or staff member and his or her ministry investment in the community. With the elders and new search committee present simply to listen respectfully (without debate, opposing comments, or "why" questions), the departing leader could be asked to respond to the following types of questions:

1. How was our church family different from what you expected when you first came?

2. How are we as leaders different from what you expected when you first came?
3. What do you perceive to be our main strengths?
4. What changes do you believe our church body should make?
5. Were there any goals you had hoped to accomplish but didn't?
6. What would have helped you accomplish those goals?
7. What agenda do you think we should complete before we call a new pastor?
8. How do you perceive your relationship with this church family after you leave?
9. Is there anything else you would like to share with us?

This is not a time for recrimination, argument, or hashing out issues. After all, the leader has already decided to leave. Although feathers might be ruffled and some of what the leader says might be hard to swallow, the purpose and benefit of an exit interview is for the remaining leaders to learn from this experience and make necessary course corrections before a new leader is brought into the church. Don't shortcut the exit interview process by skipping the praise, prayer, and encouragement steps. These vital components lay the groundwork for the question and answer phase and set the tone for the entire meeting.

After the exit interview has been completed, the church leaders should schedule a time for the congregation to bid farewell to the departing leader and family, either as part of a regular worship service or in a separate gathering called for this specific purpose. During the open meeting with the congregation, the church leaders should bless the departing leader and the departing leader should bless the church leaders. Even if your church has not used this practice, I strongly encourage that this meeting should end with a ceremony of commissioning prayer and blessing, with the laying on of hands (Acts 13:1–3). If this biblical action is minimized or ignored, a healthy leadership transition will be hampered.

Strategic Prayer During Vulnerable Transitions

Another key to achieving a successful leadership transition is bathing the process in prayer. Eighty percent of the seminary alumni and pastors in our research cited a lack of effective prayer strategies in the transition process, both for the churches and the leaders. In my experience, we have implemented the exhortation of Jesus that "My house shall be a house of prayer . . ." by organizing well-conceived corporate prayer gatherings.

If regular corporate prayer is not already a part of your church's experience, consider scheduling a "concert of prayer" as a rallying point for the congregation. See appendix 1 for a model format that has been used successfully. These prayer gatherings can be continued on a monthly or quarterly basis after the new leader has arrived, but they are especially important and beneficial during the leadership transition process. Prayer will become increasingly significant for your church family as it experiences the healing of God's presence for the grief they feel in losing a beloved staff member or pastor. Corporate prayer also fosters a greater sense of security and trust in the present church leaders, as they demonstrate their concern for the church's protection and welfare by establishing the priority of prayer. The result is that the people of God will sense the church is on a good track as it searches for a new leader.

For those ministries that have experienced an unhealthy transition, or where past issues might contaminate the opportunity for a new beginning, a more intense corporate prayer strategy may be required. Following the guidelines given by Neil Anderson and Miles Mylander in their book *Setting Your Church Free,* the leaders should set apart a retreat time for reflection and prayer.[3] According to the model of Jesus' address to the churches in Revelation 2–3, this prayer retreat would seek to discern the Lord's present view of their church by prayerfully asking:

> What if the Lord were to write a letter to our church?
> What would He commend? What would He rebuke?
> What painful memories or corporate sins have become
> part of our history that we need to corporately repent of
> and receive healing to begin anew?

After one such weekend of reflective prayer, the remaining staff and leaders of a large congregation seeking a new pastor asked me to lead a concert of prayer in their church on a Sunday morning. During a time of corporate repentance and renunciation, several leaders came to the microphone to express what God had shown them the day before. "It was as if the ceiling was removed and the sun broke through to shine all over us," said several people afterward. "Looking back on it now, we realize it was a turning point for us in letting go of our painful past. Now we are ready to face our future." Eight months later, this church was thriving with a new unity, a new pastor, and a new momentum.

Ted Engstrom, speaking at a convention of the National Association of Evangelicals, told pastors and church leaders: "One of the most important legacies a leader can give or leave the institution is a smooth transition in leadership, where the organizational alliance can be quickly and readily given to the new leader."[4] This can be done more effectively when churches communicate regularly with trusted intercessors during this critical transition time. Men and women called to the ministry of prayer and the office of intercessor should be recruited both within the church and in regional, national, or denominational intercession networks.

One pastor confessed his relief when he said, "I never asked for intercessors for myself, because I felt that it was too self-seeking. Somehow, I thought that everyone would want someone to pray for them, so why should I take advantage of my position by asking for myself? Now I realize how I had denied my potential intercessors and myself. I'm so glad that I have been delivered from such shortsightedness!"[5]

In addition to your in-house efforts, do not hesitate to ask for prayer from sister churches in your city or area. It is in the interest of every other evangelical church in your community that your church should prosper by choosing the right leadership.[6] Of course, if you expect them to pray, you must communicate updates on a regular basis. Remember, prayer is the real work; ministry is the reward or privilege that results.

One church that I assisted was without a pastor for almost two years, yet it remained strong and healthy. Several of the elders and ministry directors initiated and led prayer strategies that impacted both their church and the surrounding church community. In fact, several area churches developed long-term relationships with the new pastor and staff as a result of taking "ownership" by helping to pray in the new leader during the long period of transition.

The most critical time in a relay race is when the baton is passed from one runner to another. Our research has shown that certain issues commonly affect the volatility of leadership transitions:

- *Church Polity* issues: Independent churches with authoritarian leadership run the greatest risk of friction as they seek to integrate new leaders into the staff or replace a prominent pastor.
- *Church Age* issues: Older, established churches present a complicated mix of expectations for new leaders, and comparisons with former long-term leaders are inevitable.
- *Founding Pastor Dynamics* issues: Unless careful steps are taken

in the transition process, most new pastors who follow a founding pastor serve only as temporary transition leaders.

- *Spiritual Condition* issues: When a pastor resigns due to breakdown or personal discouragement, or retires, he often leaves behind a church that has become weak, defeated, and introspective.
- *Building Program and Debt* issues: Debt may seriously complicate the transition process by undermining the congregation's confidence and trust in leadership, especially when the one who led them into debt left soon after the building program was completed.
- *Proximity of the Predecessor* issues: If the departing leader stays in the area (especially if he has retired), loyal parishioners may have difficulty "leaving" the old leader's style and "cleaving" to the new leader's style and personality.

I have heard countless stories about how each of these issues knocked the wind out of incoming leaders whose ministry experience was running rather smoothly up until the difficult transition. Some dropped the baton and took years to recover. Others dropped out of the race completely, never to return to ministry again.

During the first three months of one new pastor's leadership, some of the charter members of the church began to complain to the former pastor, who still lived nearby. Feeling compassion for the disappointments of his close friends, he mistakenly intervened. He regrettably became involved in pressuring the elder board to remove the new pastor. If this former pastor had not been so accessible and visible to this church in transition, the congregation might have found a solution with much less dissension and pain.

Keep Your Group in the Loop

Another way that churches drop the baton is by not keeping the congregation informed about the progress of the search for a new pastor or leader. Too many churches compound the sin of prayerlessness with the sin of under-communication. Remember, when the church is in transition, everyone who attends the church is also in transition. Making your congregation feel a part of the search process is every bit as important as adequate closure and a proper send-off for the departing pastor. In the coming chapters, you will receive information about critical components of the search process. I urge you to distribute prayer requests and other information to your congregation—with regular updates—on each of these areas. Leadership transition is no time to drop the baton.

Questions for Reflection

1. What is the impact on the future of your church if you make sure that a departing leader is allowed and encouraged to leave honorably? How can the remaining leaders provide adequate opportunity for the congregation to express their love and appreciation? Have you seen examples of other churches that have handled these two steps well?

2. How can the remaining church leaders promote healing within the body after a difficult relationship with a former pastor? What is the proper role of the new leader in helping the church come to grips with its past?

3. How can your congregation develop or enhance its own ministry of prayer? Are other churches in your area known for prayer? How can their experience help you during this key transition time?

4. How can your congregation tie into the current prayer movement that is impacting other American churches? In addition to the books mentioned in this chapter, how can your church develop resources for implementing strategic prayer?

5. Research: Do any churches in your area have a history of good leadership succession? What have they done well? What have they learned from their mistakes? Reflection: How can their experience be applied in your situation?

PART TWO

MODELS AND METHODS FOR THE CHURCH

CHAPTER 3

SEARCH COMMITTEES
Choosing the Right People

S erving on a pastoral search committee is an opportunity for great personal growth, as you come to a deeper dependence on God in prayer and His Word, and gain a growing respect for the work of the Holy Spirit in the body of Christ. It may be the most significant occasion you will have to shape the future of your church or ministry.

The pastoral or leadership search committee will seek to uncover the depths of a candidate's character and calling. In the process of preparing for this important "gatekeeping" responsibility, committee members will delve deep into each other's lives. They will become the community expression of the larger church body as they relate to one another and to the candidate. This is a task for mature, seasoned believers, not novices. The first priority of prayer, then, is to determine who should serve on the pulpit or search committee.

Leith Anderson, the author of *Dying for Change,* speaks prophetically to the issue of choosing the search committee wisely and prayerfully.

> We depend on God to direct us to the leader of His choos-
> ing and we work hard to find that leader. . . . Every
> member of the search committee must faithfully ask for
> God's help. The relationships of those in the search pro-
> cess must reflect biblical principles of fellowship, in-
> tegrity, and love. It may be necessary for the search
> committee members to spend months building their own

> spiritual lives and interpersonal relationships before they
> can productively move on to the actual search. Depen-
> dence on God means faithfulness to biblical standards
> of leadership. The characteristics of leaders listed in 1
> Timothy 3 and Titus 1 cannot be ignored. . . .[1]

Individuals who are chosen for the search committee should be willing to covenant together in a support, encouragement, and accountability relationship for this ministry. It is recommended that your church
leadership create a covenant document for this purpose. One model is
presented for you in appendix 2.

In many churches, search committees are made up of representatives
from the most significant groups in the congregation, including youth
and women. Members are chosen to ensure that the interests of their
specific groups are considered, or because they have an ability to lobby
for their constituency. Many times, however, these good people have
underdeveloped listening, questioning, or assessment skills. Typically,
as many as 95 percent of the search committee's members have never
taken on such a role before, and most never will again. If not carefully
managed, a search conducted by a committee formed according to this
old paradigm will result in disillusionment for the committee members
and shipwreck for the new candidate and the church body.

---

*Thirty-eight percent of our respondents said that
some of the members of the church committees
that interviewed them seemed frustrated with
their work and portrayed a lack of clarity in
the way they interacted with one another.*

In one church that I served as an assistant pastor, the non-staff search
committee operated for more than a year without any communication
with the present staff during the search for a senior pastor. The fine person they eventually chose was never told about the small group values
that the present staff had developed and communicated to the congregation. Somehow the search committee failed to articulate these values in
the candidating process. To the incoming pastor's disappointment, and
to the detriment of the church, his philosophy of ministry turned out to
be a mismatch that could easily have been avoided.

The new paradigm for church leadership transition is to begin with the right makeup of the search committee. One method is for the elders and/or senior staff to take on this role themselves, on the assumption that those who will be partnering with the new leader can best assess issues of relational "chemistry" and team ministry skills. The old paradigm rationale for not including other pastors or senior staff on the search committee usually has something to do with the presumed benefit of "objectivity" that is gained by using non-staff individuals. However, the need to protect the flock is heightened during times when potentially unhealthy leaders may assume positions that could wound or "fleece" the flock. Church administrative systems that bypass the involvement of seasoned leaders in the selection of new leaders could place the church in a vulnerable situation. The possibility of a ministry mismatch grows whenever input from the present staff is sidestepped or ignored.

If your church polity does not allow for pastors, staff members, or other leaders to participate on the search committee, then I recommend that your leaders prayerfully choose the search committee and designate who will fill the crucial role of chairperson. The chairperson for this four- to eighteen-month process must be a well-respected, high-energy, decisive, and persistent person. In addition to presiding at the regular committee meetings, the chairperson will devote hours to developing the church profile, checking references, making phone calls, corresponding, and—possibly—traveling.

Questions for Selecting a Search Committee

The following questions will help your church leaders select the search committee:

1. Who in the church has a worthy track record in recruiting the right workers, lay leaders, or staff members?
2. Who in the church has experience in hiring, managing personnel, or consulting in the business or educational community?
3. Who in the church has experience counseling or mentoring clergy and their spouses? Who understands the unique pressures and dynamics in a minister's family?
4. Who in the church has demonstrated spiritual sensitivity and giftedness in prayer or discernment?
5. Who in the church is gifted in setting priorities, managing time,

and attending to details in the collection and preparation of information? These skills will be important for collecting and evaluating reports from denominational leaders, other church search
committees, past church references on candidates, and other sources
of important data in the committee's search.

6. Who in the church understands the need and methodology for developing a church profile that articulates the church's core values
and expectations?

7. Who in the church can pray for extended seasons, especially during crucial times of seeking clarity from the Lord?

If your church is not part of a denomination or has no ongoing meaningful relationship with other church leaders or a presbytery, then consider this proposal: Seek out two or three staff members from "kindred
spirit" churches or ministries in your area who will help you determine
the right process and secure the right person. These "outside consultants" may be able to give you key advice at vulnerable moments along
the way. They may also be willing to meet with you and help you in the
critical questioning process when you interview prospects.

Sound radical? Not according to the late Paul Bilheimmer, whose
pivotal book *Destined for the Throne* proposes that the greatest hindrance
to ministry within a city is the disunity and lack of love among its pastors. In place of competition, some now predict a growing cooperation
in the next few years among churches in the same community. Your new
pastor may come to town with a dual passion to work within your local
church and to partner with other like-minded churches to reach your city
for Christ. The time has come to recognize this emerging twenty-first-
century reality.

---

*The willingness and ability of a pastoral candi-
date to work in harmony with the staff of other
area churches will become an important criteria in the call to a local church or ministry.*

One church called me after hearing about my plans for this book and
asked me for help in choosing their new search committee. In previous
pastoral searches, they had simply drafted representatives from the major group interests within the church. This time, they have a committee

made up of eager and gifted people, who are bringing in local pastors and leaders to help them throughout their deliberations.

Short-Term Strategy

The most common reason for recruitment mistakes is summed up in this unfortunate statement: *We were in a hurry to find a pastor.* If the pressure is on and time appears to be of the essence, I strongly urge your church to consider enlisting a part-time or full-time interim pastor. These dedicated servants can relieve the search committee from the burden of worrying about the immediate pastoral needs of the congregation and give the committee adequate time to develop the strategies described in the next few chapters. A seasoned interim pastor can also help prepare the way for the people to receive their new pastor. This role is especially helpful if the church has experienced serious conflict or if the search has resulted from the departure of a long-term pastor.

Warning: The church and the interim pastor must have a clear understanding about whether the interim will be considered as a prospective candidate. Normally the interim pastor should not be considered as a candidate for the following reasons:

1. By virtue of working within the church, the interim pastor gains an unfair advantage over other candidates who will not have the same visibility. The goal of the search committee is to find the individual who best fits the profile of the church. They might be tempted to adapt the profile to match the style of the interim pastor.
2. The interim pastor has a unique opportunity to lead in ways that might not be received from a permanent pastor.
3. An interim pastor will always have those who are for him and those who are against him. Whether or not he is chosen as the new pastor, some in the church will be upset, resulting in unnecessary conflict. Also, if he is not chosen, his feelings about not being selected could hinder the remainder of his ministry until the new pastor arrives.

With a clearly defined job description in writing, and an agreed-upon period of service, the right interim pastor can serve as the "bridge over troubled waters" for both the search committee and the church family, allowing the church to move forward with the important work of the courtship process.

Long-Term Strategy

As soon as the church leaders have appointed a chairperson and committee members, a full framework for the committee's work should be established. The following key elements should be included:

1. Set meeting agendas for the next four to fifteen months, including saturation times of prayer.
2. Complete a self-study of the ministry to identify present conditions, needs, and future goals.
3. Arrange for an interim pastor and/or additional lay leadership to fill the gaps left by the departing leader.
4. Develop a church profile (see chapter 4).
5. Determine potential compensation packages for candidates.
6. Begin the search for potential candidates.
7. Contact potential candidates to determine levels of interest.
8. Visit the churches of the most promising candidates.
9. Winnow the list of prospects and check the references of the remaining candidates.
10. Communicate appreciation and regrets to those who do not meet committee criteria.
11. Conduct interviews with the top candidates.
12. Communicate regular updates to existing staff and the congregation.
13. Negotiate a tentative call and terms with the preferred candidate.
14. Arrange for the candidate to spend quality time with the church board and parishioners, including preaching and ministering opportunities.
15. Enable the church to confirm a potential call to the top candidate.
16. Notify the candidates who are not confirmed.
17. Notify the candidate who is confirmed, acquire acceptance of the call, and determine the starting date.
18. Announce the acceptance and the starting date to the church.
19. Welcome the new pastoral family.
20. Send letters of thanks to all who helped in the search.
21. Dissolve the search committee and take a well-deserved vacation!

Another way of picturing this overall process is to put it in terms of the key challenges that have to be faced at each stage of the search:

1. Start appropriately, building on a foundation of prayer.
2. Identify and select the right people for the search committee.

3. Identify key interim issues and allocate resources to stay the course.
4. Establish the search team and develop unity and community within the committee.
5. Build correctly by determining a strategic plan of action.
6. Look honestly at candidates by gathering the necessary data.
7. Keep perspective by focusing on the big picture.
8. Answer the hard questions by addressing your church's issues.
9. Profile the right person by determining your criteria.
10. Choose wisely through prayer, discernment, and consensus.
11. Cultivate candidates by locating and evaluating prospects.
12. Present the scope of the job and the nature of the church's culture realistically to candidates by interacting effectively and authentically.
13. Decide the process for determining God's direction and come to an agreement.
14. Finish effectively by ensuring the proper beginning for the new leader.
15. Complete all the tasks and follow-up responsibilities.

As the members of the committee begin to understand the complexity of the search process, they will need the support of the church in prayer and encouragement. At times, individual members will feel overwhelmed by the responsibility. At other times they might feel intimidated by the degree of detailed effort required. The requirement of confidentiality alone may affect normal relations with fellow church members or their own spouses, resulting in confusion and even anger. These seasons of emotional upheaval must be shared within the fellowship of the search committee. This level of support and intimacy will not be possible if the committee hasn't focused on becoming a community.

Learning to laugh together, especially at the beginning of this potentially stressful process, encourages community life. Share with the committee some of the cartoons published over the years in *Leadership* magazine. They are excellent at pinpointing the lighter side of the issues that all search committees face in their work.

Another way to create a relaxed and friendly atmosphere for the committee's proceedings is to meet somewhere other than a sterile, tile-floored, fluorescent-lit Sunday school room in the back of a dark and empty church building. Meet in someone's home and have a potluck together. After all, doesn't the Bible tell us to "buffet our bodies"!

Preparation Research Data

Our survey of alumni from Bible schools and seminaries, who had either served on a search committee or had been interviewed by a search committee, revealed the following insights that every new search committee should discuss in its preliminary meetings:

1. Many search committees are *inexperienced* (37%) in the selection process. Most are made up of diverse personalities who have been thrown together with little direction and few guidelines and told to perform a specific task in a short time. The average chairperson has little experience in facilitating community relationships but may have strong task-driven skills.

2. *Unrealistic or unexpressed expectations* (25%) from the congregation often result in wrong selections. The expectations voiced by the committee during the interview may have been watered down to get the position filled. After the pastor has been hired, the congregation may expect him to meet certain values that were not clearly expressed during the process. When the new pastor sees that the church's expectations do not match the expectations expressed by the committee, he often leaves.

3. Many search committees are *overly anxious to fill the position* (23%). Members often portray a lack of excitement about the task and responsibility and even appear to resent the time they have to spend on the committee. The prevailing attitude seems to be, "Let's get this over with and go home."

4. Selection committees often *rely on human wisdom rather than divine guidance* (16%). If the candidate looks good, says the right things, and has good references, he often gets the job, even though important elements of his personality or philosophy of ministry don't fit the church. The selection process is often perceived as a "one-shot deal," with little or no time for intercessory prayer by which to discern the will of God.

5. Search committees are often *uncertain of the church's real needs* (12%). Church leaders complain that the needs expressed at the interview by the committee are really not the actual needs of the church. Either the church leaders have not adequately assessed their needs, or they have not shared this information with the search committee.

These conclusions were based on the highest percentage of similar comments given in response to our research questions.

Questions for Discussion

1. Have you ever served on a search committee? How were you chosen? What changes would you recommend in the selection process?
2. What are some advantages and disadvantages of having an interim pastor? Do you know of situations where the interim pastor helped the search committee in its strategic planning?
3. How could the results of our research influence your church in the selection and work of the search committee?

CHAPTER 4

YOUR CHURCH PROFILE
Clarifying Core Values

"Prior to candidating for this position, I put together a
packet that represented who I am and my theological per-
spectives. I was very thorough. I later found out that none
of the search committee evaluated this information in
detail. Even when I pulled out key points in my packet to
challenge them, they all seemed to agree with my positions. You see, they were hungry for a pastor at the time.
It didn't matter where I stood, they wanted me. Now that
I've been hired, things are different. One of the key elders criticizes every change and opposes anything that
doesn't originate from his own lips. It seems that every
pastor I talk to in my area lately gives me sympathy and
support. Even in a city of two hundred thousand, they all
knew about this guy. As a prominent businessman and
elder, he made his mark long before I accepted this call."

Good marital preparation requires that couples get in touch with the
spoken and unspoken values, traditions, and expectations that each brings
to the marriage. Sometimes, looking at a family's history reveals a lot
about a person's values. I remember surprising one young couple by
suggesting that one of the best things they could do to prepare for their
upcoming marriage was to move in with each other's parents for a while
(the bride with his folks, the groom with her folks) to discover how their

future in-laws treated each other. They didn't take me up on it, but I'm sure the idea made them stop and think about how likely they were to treat each other the same way their parents had modeled. It helped them to understand why they were doing what they were doing. The same dynamics operate inside the church, and a pastoral candidate can learn a lot by spending time with his future "family."

Core Values Clarification

"Family values" has become a common phrase in today's cultural battle for the soul of our nation. "Core values" will be a common phrase in tomorrow's spiritual battle for the soul of our churches. In the search for new leaders, core values are a useful indicator because they reveal more than a church's printed vision or mission statement or a candidate's standard résumé. Mission statements and résumés tend to answer the questions, "What are we doing?" or "What have we done?" A statement of core values, on the other hand, answers the question, *"Why* are we doing what we're doing?" Values statements are more constant than vision or mission statements, and they evoke more passion from the people who own them.

Seventy-two percent of our respondents said that either they or the prospective church did not clearly communicate their core values during the candidating process.

Church leaders spend too much energy coming up with marketing phrases to encapsulate their church's vision, which is then printed in the bulletin but not emblazoned in their hearts. Proverbs 7:1–3 exhorts us to write the Lord's words and His commandments (His core values, if you will) on the tablets of our hearts. Most mission statements don't resonate at the core level of the human heart. They don't evoke the passionate response of the Emmaus Road disciples who exclaimed, "Were not our hearts burning within us while he talked with us on the road and opened the Scriptures to us?" Discovering your ministry's core values involves much more than coming up with a catchy commercial jingle for promotional purposes. It is really a matter of seeking to discover the heart of your leadership and your ministry. Jack Hayford gives us a prophetic warning about this heart issue when he says,

Nothing is more chic in today's management technique than answering the present mandate that every corporation project a concise mission and vision statement, with a companion set of "core values." . . . Whatever the church's mission, in the final analysis, the character of the leadership will determine its fruit. The "heart" will be the final measure of success, whatever else may have been achieved.[1]

Importance of Core Values

In his book called *Values Driven Leadership*, Aubrey Malphurs suggests a number of key reasons why discovering core values is an important role for church leaders.

1. Values discovery and clarification empowers a ministry to know its distinctives.
2. Values communicate what is really important to a church or ministry organization.
3. Values help determine what changes will be helpful or harmful to a ministry.
4. Values inspire people to action and generate deeper personal involvement in the life of the members and employees.
5. Leaders who reinforce a church's values connect with the people on a gut level and cause them to sense a "kindred spirit" with the leader or candidate.[2]

What is crucial here is to define and articulate the *actual* core values of the church or ministry organization, not the *aspirational* values. For example, we must look at what our parishioners actually *do* about the poor and the lost, not what they *intend* to do, or believe they *should* do, or *think* they are doing. It is essential that we genuinely evaluate ourselves in this process and not try to put the best light on a situation where nothing is really happening. The search committee can begin by writing down what they believe are the church's values and then they should conduct a "values audit" on the congregation itself. See appendix 3 for an example of the values audit process.

The church leadership team at New Life Christian Fellowship in Chesapeake, Virginia, did their homework and came up with a list of core values that represented the corporate input of the church body. They identified the following key values, among others:

- *Overall Balance:* Our church is a place where balance, authenticity, integrity, and excellence should permeate every area of church life and relationship. Meeting people's needs should be more important than maintaining programs.
- *Genuine Relationships:* Our church is a place where healthy and loving relationships are considered indispensable to spiritual formation and growth. We should relate to each other as a multiethnic, multicultural blend of God's people, whose focus is not on social, economic, racial, or gender distinctions, but rather on the beauty of expressing God through a diverse body of believers.
- *Worship and Prayer:* Our church is a place where there is a commitment to exuberant and celebrative worship (free but always orderly), to the expression of spiritual gifts (to build up the body and evangelize the lost), and to continual prayer (both intimate and strategic). Worship should never surrender to fanaticism, spiritual gifts should never violate Scripture, and expressed joy should never degenerate into infectious excitability.
- *Servant Leadership:* Our church is a place where there is shared ministry among a team of leaders. While the church should be led by those who have demonstrated godly character and integrity, and clearly possess leadership gifts, servanthood is the goal of all leadership and ministry.
- *Cross-Cultural Missions:* Our church is a place where the cause of world evangelism is vigorously and faithfully pursued with a commitment to ministering cross-culturally—especially among the unreached peoples of the world. All believers should be world-class Christians, having a heart to share Christ with cultures other than their own.
- *Christian Self-Image:* Our church is a place where believers understand that they cannot earn God's acceptance, but are freely accepted because of the finished work of Jesus Christ. Therefore, the church should never utilize guilt nor legalism to motivate its members, but rather should encourage them to live godly lives purely motivated by their lives for God.

How does a church come up with such a list of values? In this particular fellowship, the pastors and elders worked through their own ideas over a period of months before presenting them to the congregation. In another effective church, the leadership core gathered 60 percent of the congregation, who were already functioning in cells (small groups), to facilitate the discussion and make notes of what they believed were their church's core values. After collecting all the suggested values within a cell, each group prioritized their ideas into a list of the top five. Each of the cells then brought their top five values to the larger group discussion, and a facilitator helped the church compile a final list.

Criteria for Good Values

The values expressed by New Life Christian Fellowship are worthy examples because they meet the top four criteria for determining good core values. First and foremost, they are biblical. Each value can be represented by a Scripture passage, not because a Bible verse was tacked on to support the value, but because there was a corporate sense that God was illuminating these particular passages in the life of the church.

Second, these are good values because they touch our passions. This may sound like a dangerous concept to those of us who were reared on a heavy dose of "left brain infosermons," as some of my baby buster church members put it. The point is that core values affect the spiritual center of our personal and corporate lives because they make sense to us intellectually, grip us emotionally, and inspire us to concrete action or changes in behavior.

Third, these are good values because they are shared by the core of committed workers and leaders in this church congregation. The people who end up working together are attracted to each other because they share the same core values. The joy of "partnership in the gospel" that Paul talks about in Philippians 1 encompasses the special sense of significance and accomplishment that comes through partnering with others who share similar core values.

Fourth, these are good values because they will stand the test of time. They have a sense of constancy about them that won't rise or fall on the personal preferences of this year's elder board chairman. No matter what happens in the world or surrounding community, these values represent a steady definition of the congregation's view of the kingdom of God on earth as expressed through this ministry.

After years of watching those I have trained rise and fall on ministry battlefields, I have arrived at a basic conclusion. Our emerging leaders don't need more exegetical or theological training. Instead, they must develop the ability to understand culture, particularly church culture. The bottom line for any pastoral candidate is to be able to discern "the□way we do things around here." Many of the most difficult issues in the life of a leader and the church are not "spiritual issues" per se. The stumbling blocks are more often related to values—whether spoken, written, or merely assumed but hidden. These values may be expressed in a combination of norms, rituals, expectations, hero stories, boundaries, and traditions. Whatever we call them, we need to know that every individual operates according to internal values, and every group of individuals (such as a business or a church congregation) operates according to internalized corporate values that determine its corporate identity.

Over the years, I have assigned some of my students the task of trying to discover a church's values without referring to any of its written documents. The project appears difficult until the students learn to switch their focus from what the church *says* about itself to what the church actually *does*. They begin to look at what the leaders are modeling in their lives as well as what they are preaching and teaching in their messages. For instance, if pastors preach about responsibility to the lost and the poor, and if they teach about cooperation between parts of the body, are the leaders actually spending time with the lost or the poor, and are they working cooperatively with other city leaders, or are they only giving lip service to these values, saying they are good ones to have?

My students also listen to conversations within the church body—formal, prayerful, and informal—to see what is being communicated. Sometimes, stories about the church's past and present are the main vehicle for passing on what was really important to the members. Ultimately, a church's budget (where they spend their money) and its programs (where they spend their time) make statements about the church's *actual* values, as opposed to those that are only *aspirational*. Core values have always influenced the direction of churches, but often we look in the wrong places to see what they are.

The Lure of Church Planting

Some leaders might find the process of discerning a congregation's values too tedious and involved. They just want to get on with the business of advancing the kingdom and might choose the excitement of church planting over the task of analyzing an existing church's value system. Some leaders move toward church planting because they hold values that are not readily expressed in existing churches. Others may take on the challenge of church planting after failing to do their values-discovery homework in past churches. After a couple of painful experiences of ministry mismatch at the level of values, some may want to be their own boss in a new start-up. One of the attractive aspects of a start-up is that the leader's core values will establish the foundation for the new church's corporate values. Yet if they skip over the exercise of values clarification and communication, these leaders may find themselves in the same kind of mismatch three or four years down the road. After all, it takes at least a few members to start up a new work, and these people bring their own expectations and values to the church. Even in a new church, the congregation will push and pull in ways that may conflict with the leader's personal values. Ultimately, the emerging body will congregate around certain common values, and these will become the *de facto* values of that congregation. The leader may feel the pressure to leave again when he realizes he is in another mismatched relationship. However, if the leader or leaders of a start-up church clearly define and communicate the church's core values, and these values are *practiced*—not merely talked about— newcomers to the church will decide whether they fit within the congregation, and the chances for a mismatch will be diminished.

Questions for Discussion

1. In what ways is your church distinctive? Which key values determine or illustrate these distinctions?
2. Is your ministry or church in a state of decline, growth, or plateau? In what way do your core values reinforce this trend?
3. What values does your church have written down or regularly talk about? What values does the congregation hold on a subconscious level?
4. Write down all of the values you have discovered about your ministry organization. How many of these pass the test of good values (biblical, passionate, shared, timeless)?

CHAPTER 5

HEART ISSUES

Determining Your Church's Readiness for Change

"I feel you imposed this change without getting my input or consent."

"My routine has been disrupted."

"I'm afraid of where we're headed."

"You haven't given me any reasons to make these changes."

"I'm basically satisfied with the way things are right now."

"You mean everything we did in the past
doesn't count around here anymore?"

"It's a lot of work to start something new again."

Change is costly. During their time in the wilderness, the children of Israel grew so weary of change that they were willing to go back to the bondage of Egypt, with its familiar leeks and onions, rather than continue on to the land of Canaan. The process of change involves grieving over the loss of the familiar and anxiety over the unknown future. Some church cultures are more responsive to change than others, and certain changes can be very unsettling to the relationships of leaders and followers.

Church leaders can be effective "change agents," but only if they understand how the church, its ministry systems, and its core values function together. Dr. Ralph Neighbor has compiled decades of research from traditional churches whose core values and program-based structures underwent radical transitions. Case studies from these vibrant and authentic New Testament communities, which take evangelism and discipleship seriously, support the following conclusion: It takes six experiences to change someone's values. These experiences must include feedback and learning in order to establish a deep change in a core value.

It would be interesting to do a detailed Scripture study to examine this conclusion. For instance, we could research how Jesus developed specific core values in His disciples. Dr. Neighbor reminds us that we could read all of the recorded content of Jesus' teaching in less than an hour if it was compiled in one document. The rest of the recorded life of Jesus focuses on what He did—the real-life episodes in which Jesus mobilized His small group of disciples, often repeating Himself and re-emphasizing a truth (or core value) through a variety of parables, lessons, and hands-on experiences. These encounters were designed to expose the disciples' core values and replace them with the radical values of the kingdom.

Taking Your Church's Pulse

In order to determine how open your church is to accepting the changes that might be initiated by a new pastor or staff member, three key areas must be examined:

Number One: Identify how new proposals are normally handled in the church. New wine needs new wineskins. If all new ideas have to go through the bottleneck of a standing board or committee, then there will be great resistance to change. Lyle Schaller puts it well:

> When someone proposes a new idea, decide how it should be handled. If you want it rejected, refer it to a standing committee. If you decide it needs refining and improving, send it to a special study committee. If it has obvious merit and deserves to be implemented, create a special ad hoc committee and direct its members to turn that new proposal into reality.[1]

Number Two: Determine which category each of the key influencers in the church falls into: early adopters, middle adopters, later adopters, and never adopters. Key influencers are those people, with or without a title, to whom others go for advice. They are the members of the congregation whose opinions hold sway with others.

The key group to consider in this model is the middle adopters, which may describe as much as 80 percent of the congregation. Middle adopters are those who "need to see it to believe it." Middle adopters want to see some proof before they'll go along with a new idea. An incoming pastor who wants to bring about change within the church must take the middle adopters into account and structure the change in ways that meet their need for evidence. Are any of the existing staff in this category? Do most of the key leaders in the church fall into this category?

Church size and the flexibility of its leaders are key ingredients in the tendency of a congregation to resist or receive innovation and change. One of my former colleagues accepted a call to a church that had dwindled from seven hundred to seventy members. The remaining parishioners were so desirous for any change that would help that they readily agreed to accept the leadership initiatives my colleague suggested as their new pastor. Five years later, the church had grown to nine hundred members and had planted several churches. My friend told me that this church had demonstrated the kind of desperation he looked for when evaluating a new pastoral opportunity. They were responsive to change because they had run out of options!

Lyle Schaller agrees that churches in decline that are aware of their problems are more open to change, even though it brings accompanying stress. Plateaued churches with less than two hundred members usually have a more resistant core of middle to late adopters. Schaller thinks that it might take five to eight years before these churches will allow the leader to lead most effectively in the change process. When you consider that the average stay of a staff pastor in a church is two and one-half to three and one-half years, it's easy to see that many of these pastors are leaving in frustration before they have a chance to accomplish their objectives. And as I mentioned earlier, an alarming percentage of them are dropping out of the ministry entirely. How much better it would be for everyone if these pastors could match the church's readiness for change with their own willingness to lead the change process. Armed with this information, they might be more open to stay long enough to bring about the needed modifications in a church.

Number Three: Conduct a "readiness for change inventory" with your congregation to help pastoral candidates determine whether their gifts for leading change match the responsiveness level of the church body. See appendix 4 for a sample of a readiness for change inventory. The goal here is to identify how much your congregation will help or hinder the incoming leader's efforts to promote change.

In Aubrey Malphurs's excellent discussion of change, he identifies why people resist it.[2] If you were to ask the members of your congregation to produce a list of their felt needs, "change" would probably not be on the list. Most churches seek to maintain a sense of "constancy" amid the swirling seas of societal change all around. Without a "divine dissatisfaction," most people don't feel a need to change.

A second reason that a church body might resist change is because they can't see how their core values will be affirmed by the changes. Proponents of innovative church strategies, such as the cell church movement, caution pastors against leading their traditional churches too rapidly into a transition. Research shows that it takes three to five years to change values in a church body. If that is the case, it would be wise to begin with changes that do not require a change in values and to give adequate attention to reinforcing existing values before implementing other changes.

People also resist change when forms have become more sacred than functions. The old rule of thumb from architecture—"form follows function"—applies to the church as well. A function such as evangelism is an absolute value and an intrinsic part of the life and purpose of every evangelical church. But the forms, the particular ways that we do evangelism (such as annual revivals, street ministry, door-to-door canvassing), are relative and should be changed periodically to keep our ministry "culturally relevant." In *Say No, Say Yes to Change,* Elaine Dickinson warns us about assigning a sacred quality to things that are not intrinsically sacred. Whenever something becomes a "sacred cow," it becomes immune to change. Sometimes these sacred cows are positions of prestige that have become vested interests for certain people in the ministry organization.

The search committee should be able to show a candidate concrete examples of how changes occurred under the leadership of former pastors. The candidate should be told how, when, and why people were resistant to these changes. To shield this valuable information from pastoral candidates may prove costly for both the church and the new pastor.

After I graduated from seminary, I spent my early years of ministry as an associate pastor in a good, mentoring relationship with a wise pastor. This relationship continued when I soloed as a senior pastor, bringing a culturally conservative church into some rapid and unsettling changes during my first eighteen months. Some of the changes we made were adding praise and worship choruses; launching a ministry to prisons, with convicts visiting our church on weekend leaves; founding a ministry to French-speaking Canadians within our culturally prejudiced English-speaking church; and using drama and the arts in our worship time. Before long, even some of my finest elders were reeling. One of them came to me and pleaded, "Pastor, everything around me is changing: my job, my community, my family, my world. The church is the one place I come to get in touch with something constant. But every Sunday I have to face something new. I don't think I can handle much more change."

It was then that I made a decision to commit myself for the long haul and work through the church's resistance to change. Over the next five years, we solidified several of the initial major changes before initiating more innovations. We spent considerable time confirming and reinforcing the values that were dear to the people of God in the community. We moved key leaders through a series of experiences that helped them in their own values-changing process. After six and a half years, I recognized that I did not have God's vision for taking the church into the next lengthy cycle of change. I left on a high note, and the church was able to find another leader whose skills and interests matched their revised set of needs and expectations.

For those who still think that effecting change is simply a matter of preaching a series of three-point sermons on key issues, consider these four steps to change mentioned by Reggie McNeal and several others:

1. Change in *knowledge*. The information that people need to know or understand before they will see a need for change.
2. Change in *attitude*. The attitudes people must have before they will begin to act in the desired ways.
3. Change in *individual behavior*. How will individuals need to act in order for the desired change to occur? Who will need to act differently?
4. Change in *group behavior*. How will the church climate and culture be different after the change occurs? Which groups will be called upon to change?[3]

Conducting a Truthful Self-Study

Before searching for a new pastor, the search committee cannot avoid the important foundational step of conducting a thorough self-study. If this step is skipped or glossed over, the committee runs the risk of making several crucial mistakes:

1. The congregation, pastor, and community won't fit together.
2. The search team won't identify the leader who can take them to the next growth level.
3. The church will fail to evaluate its current ministries to see if they are still relevant.

In *Choosing a New Pastor,* Henry A. Virkler makes this rather incisive observation:

> Failure to do a self-study can lead to choosing a pastor who is either exactly like the previous pastor or who is opposite, depending on whether or not you like the previous pastor.[4]

The process of completing a thorough profile takes a lot longer than most search committees envision. They must gather annual reports for the past five years, review the current annual budget and church bylaws, evaluate worship attendance reports for the past five years, and conduct an up-to-date membership survey. Appendix 6 has an example of a self-evaluation form that has been used effectively to involve church members and leaders in the development of a church profile.

In addition to clarifying core values, evaluating the congregation's readiness for change, and gathering accurate church data, the search committee should ask the following four questions to gain an accurate picture of the church as a body of believers:

1. What has been the history of the ministry's relationship with past staff members, including tenured pastors and other leaders?

Relationship patterns that become evident over time reveal the unspoken values of the church community. They also indicate the kinds of expectations that parishioners will have of new staff members. Examining these historical proclivities will bring to light unresolved hurts or bitterness left over from past leaders. Any new leader would appreciate knowing about these issues in advance.

Had I been privy to this kind of information earlier in my life, I might have avoided one of the major conflicts that almost took me out of a church in my second year. Certain behaviors of mine reminded some of the parishioners of a former leader with whom they'd had a difficult relationship. Their negative response to my leadership was a reaction to the memories and pain from the past. Fortunately, I discovered this connection before I responded in ways that would have reinforced their fearful expectations.

A major Christian ministry in the United States has a sordid history of periodically firing its employees and hiring new people to replace them. Rather than retooling and retraining good people who have given years of service as part of their sense of calling, this organization is known for its "binge and purge" mentality toward its staff. It continues to astonish me that new employees don't even ask how past employees have been treated before relocating their families across the country to take these new positions. I warn every leader who is checking out a possible position in a church or ministry organization to first find out the pattern of how past employees have been treated.

2. What kind of disciples has the ministry produced over the years? What are common emotional and character traits among paid and unpaid workers?

Every church wants to teach people how to be more like Jesus in character and behavior; yet each church emphasizes a particular way to pursue this goal. Purpose-driven churches, such as Pastor Rick Warren's Saddleback Community Church, intend to produce certain qualities in those who enter into the life of their church. This is accomplished by prayerfully defining the "profiles" of people who are part of the life of the church, such as the unique way they relate to each other, their community, and the unreached nations. Purpose-driven churches should be able to give a response to this kind of question: "If I give myself to this church for two to three years what will I look like as a result?"

By talking to people who have been around the church for a few years, a discerning search committee can identify key traits that seem to be part of their church's "DNA." Ideally, the unique aroma of Christ would so pervade committed members of a particular church that even unchurched people in the surrounding community could tell they are from the same church family. Understanding this is foundational for recognizing the pervasive role of a church's culture that will either help or hinder the work of a new pastor or leader.

3. How does the church as a whole, and its key lay leaders in particular, deal with conflict?

Research from churches across America indicates that 75–80 percent of church members choose to avoid conflict whenever possible. These results suggest that a large majority of parishioners desire and expect the church to be different from other organizations. Still, whenever human beings get together, some conflict is inevitable, and churches will develop patterns, either healthy or toxic, for how they deal with it. Over the years, unresolved conflict can create toxic strongholds that lock a church into cycles of destructive behaviors and complicated response patterns.

I have witnessed some painful church splits that divided communities and families. One devastating meeting I attended ended with four hundred people walking out to start a new church one mile down the road. What was astonishing to me was that both sides of the split thought their positions were quite reasonable! Unfortunately, it is often far too easy to establish mental strongholds—castles built in our minds through wrong beliefs, fears, and negative thoughts. The church at Laodicea honestly believed it was rich, wealthy, and self-sufficient—when in fact it was poor, wretched, miserable, and blind!

The apostle Paul exhorts us not to be ignorant of the devices of the enemy, who would like nothing better than to render the church of God ineffective. Whenever conflict occurs within the church, we can discover the toxic tendencies that are repeated over the years in church relationships. These predictable patterns may involve such detrimental behavior as withdrawal, politicking, rumor spreading, second guessing, and undermining, which become a familiar part of the church history and may appear to be normal behavior in the eyes of some of the participants. If the search committee can honestly identify these traits and present the information to a serious candidate, the church might be able to call someone who is seasoned in healthy conflict intervention, and who can pull down these strongholds and move the church to a new level of community.

4. Name other churches and church leaders who are admired.
Which ones would our church and leaders like to emulate?

It has been said that leaders are always working with two churches at the same time: the church as it is and the church as they want it to be. For many pastors, the church that is closest to their hearts is one they have read about, visited, or admired somewhere else, and they long to somehow shape their present church along the same lines. Within a church, the lay leaders and potential staff leaders have role models that they look up to that might not be revealed unless someone is sensitive enough to ask.

During a difficult season of transition in one of my churches, I heard some of my key leaders say something to this effect: "Pastor, I don't have any major problems with what you are doing now. I can accept these changes in the worship service and style of ministry. But what really concerns me is—where are we headed? Is there anyone else doing what you're proposing we do?" What they were asking was what Jesus recognized as the heart need of every disciple when He gave the invitation to "come and see." When we can describe what the church in our heart looks like—or better yet, give an example—it will help to relieve the fear of the unknown that grips many a congregation. Clarity of vision and purpose will also facilitate a ministry match by reaching and uncovering the deeper core issues.

Sixty percent of our pastoral candidate respondents told us that the search committees they had encountered had been forthright and direct with them about the church's strengths and weaknesses, and that this approach made the entire matching process a meaningful spiritual experience.

All search committees have to live with the tension between wanting to put their best foot forward in their profile and wanting to portray a realistic picture of the church. It is time for the evangelical community to err on the side of humility, honesty, and integrity in the candidating process. We cannot afford to borrow from the world's marketing strategies and only emphasize the "sizzle" in the product. Someone on the search committee must advocate the Pauline exhortation to "boast in our weakness" rather than in our strength. To do otherwise will only encourage the pastoral candidates to puff up their own strengths and disguise their weaknesses, leaving the door open for eventual disillusionment.

CHAPTER 6

INTEGRITY

Confirming the Candidate's Character

"John was a well-liked member of our pastoral staff who had initiated a number of innovations within our church over the previous year. But one day when he left the senior pastor's office, his usual smile was gone and his voice trembled. 'I can't believe the anger and disrespect he just vented on me,' he said as he packed up his office in front of us. 'My brother's secular company treats its employees with more respect than this.'

John and his wife, Christie, left the ministry that year to work for his brother. They haven't been to church since.

"The worst part of our story is that the senior pastor went on to fire more of our best leaders over the next several years. Later, after the church had split and dwindled to less than half its former size, we discovered that every church he had led in the past had experienced the same grief of losing their finest pastors because of the way this man treated them. If only someone had told us, we could have protected our church and staff from this spiritual abuse."

Key Issues That Every Church Must Examine in a Potential Leader

All search committee members should personally review the scriptural qualifications in 1 Timothy 3 and Titus 1 and make notes on the outward reputation, inner disposition, and experience level of the candidates that these verses emphasize. In the initial stage of committee meetings, a brief time should be devoted to discussing these insights and ways to identify these traits in candidates.

1. Look for Character Signs That Reveal the Issues of the Heart

Sadly, search committees tend to overlook the need for individual members to search the Scriptures to learn the character qualifications of a leader. The most often repeated survey response from pastors and pastors-to-be in our research is that search committees focus on the wrong characteristics, such as personality, appearance, poise, and charisma, rather than discerning the real heart of the person. As it says in 1 Samuel 16:7, "Man looks at the outward appearance, but the LORD looks at the heart" (NKJV). Discerning the heart of an individual is difficult, but there are several key character signs that reveal much about a leader's heart for the Lord.[1]

- *Family:* How does this leader treat his spouse and children? Does he honor, bless, affirm, and love them? Whatever behavior is evidenced here will show up in his relationships with the church family.
- *Speech Patterns:* Is this leader slow to speak and quick to hear (James 1:19)? How does he talk about others, including controversial Christian leaders?
- *Money:* How does he manage his personal and family finances? Is there a burden of heavy debt that comes from poor management of resources or poor self-management?
- *Suffering:* How does he respond to disappointment, stress, or situations that he cannot control?
- *Time:* Does he leave any "margin" in his life or is he always "pressing the edge of the envelope" in the way he approaches people or projects? Is he a good steward of his own and others' time?

Pastor and author Jack Hayford lives a life message of integrity, and many times he has openly shared his own struggle to maintain excellence of character in the unique challenge of the ministry. In addition to the standard warnings he gives to ministry leaders to avoid the "gold, glitter, and girls," more commonly known as the traps of money, self-glory, and sex, Hayford also warns against the snares of inaccuracy, privilege, power, and prestige.[2]

Matters of *accuracy:* This refers to absolute honesty in all areas of communication, especially the temptation to exaggerate attendance numbers. Much of the evangelical community is addicted to the numbers game, and pastors who resist this stronghold will seem to be out of step with some of their leaders. A search committee would be well advised to find out on which side of reality their potential leader usually errs when giving reports.

Recently, I witnessed the unfortunate termination of a very qualified person from the leadership of a large ministry. He seemed to possess an unblemished character and was a role model for many, but when his pattern of padding facts and finances in reports was uncovered, he showed no remorse. A blind spot had developed in this area of his character until he believed that his methods were standard operating procedure for all businesses and ministries. Our deceitful hearts will find every justification for the spin we put on reality.

Matters of *privilege:* For many in the ministry who struggle under the burden of limited finances, the few perks that are still available to ministers in our culture are greatly appreciated. Opting out of Social Security and/or designating some salary as a "housing allowance" have been good opportunities to realize a greater cash flow on a fixed salary.

However, when occasional privileges or financial gifts are offered by grateful parishioners, the subtle temptation for a leader is to feel that he somehow deserves them. The second temptation is to hide these gifts from others in leadership. A final temptation is for a leader to use his means of communication—from the pulpit, or otherwise—to actually manipulate or exploit others to provide special privileges. The search committee should seek to evaluate a candidate's history in this sensitive area.

The best way to help a pastor resist these temptations is to establish "real time" accountability with others on a daily basis. Another way to guard against this danger is for the church to offer its leaders generous, legitimate benefits, such as book and conference allowances, tuition for ongoing education, and paid—yes, even paid—sabbaticals outside of family vacation time. The not-so-funny joke of the church board that says, "Lord, you keep them humble, we'll keep them poor," reflects the apparent attitude of too many churches that fail to treat their leaders with the "double honor" that Scripture says they deserve. Generous churches help their leaders maintain integrity in the area of receiving privilege.

Matters of *power and prestige:* Like the guns on the battleship *Missouri,* leaders have the means to use their title, their knowledge, their vocabulary, their calling, and other gifts and abilities in ways that could potentially blow people out of the water. Leadership in ministry offers plenty of opportunities to discard the "servant leader" mandate in favor of saying, "Just this once, let me call down fire from heaven!" As the late Dr. David Hubbard observed about his own life, we should finish the race saying at the end, "I never exercised the full extent of the power inherent in my position."

Whenever a spiritual leader is tempted to act independently in a "full show of power," he should remind himself of the fine line between chastising and crushing. If we knew how many staff members have suffered from the stinging tongue and strong-arm pressure that results from this integrity issue, it would surely sober us to ask each candidate about the history of his staff relationships.

2. Assess the Candidate's Vitality in Key Areas of Spiritual Health

Worship: Leaders who are unashamed to reveal their devotion and adoration for the Lord Jesus Christ through worship will encourage parishioners in their own spiritual passion. Like the psalmist David, pastoral candidates should demonstrate evidence that they have "a heart after God." Pastors and ministry leaders should be like magnets drawing people to pursue the presence of God on a daily rather than a Sunday-morning-only basis.

Allowing for the different temperaments, talents, gifts, and styles of effective leaders, there is still no debate needed on the value of spiritual passion for Christ in the life of a leader. The questions are simple and straightforward: Is the candidate in love with Jesus? Does he love to spend time in His presence? Is there a holy and joyful desire to be in the house of the Lord worshiping corporately with God's people? Is there a contagious enthusiasm for worship that comes from interacting with this person? Does he enjoy teaching, preaching, or sharing about worship as evidence of its priority in life?

We've all heard the standard jibes about the many in our culture who have resorted to "church hopping." But perhaps we should consider the possibility that average Christians today are hungering for spiritual reality and spiritual growth, and that they are legitimately restless in many of our sleepy churches. The bottom line in far too many churches is that the leaders are not growing in spiritual passion for the person and presence of Jesus. A leader simply can't take others where he hasn't been himself—or where he once was years ago. Without an up-to-date and meaningful worship life, our leaders will model religion rather than relationship. If your prospective leader is shy about sharing his worship life, you can be certain that your people will be sadly underdeveloped in this area under his ministry.

Prayer: Leaders who pray as if they really know the ways and character of God will reveal the presence of God with their words. Their prayers will have a focus, an economy of words that will release the Word of God and build up the faith of those who hear. They will contain a passion that displays an intercessory burden for God's people. Above all, they will have an honesty and integrity about the struggles of life and faith that will cause others to identify with them and with the prayer lives of the men and women in Scripture.

Studies have revealed that the average pastor in America prays twenty-two minutes a day.[3] While determining the number of minutes your potential leader prays each day is not necessarily the best indicator of a meaningful prayer life, it is incumbent upon the church leaders to probe this critical area with each candidate. Where does he pray? How does he pray? What hindrances does he experience in prayer? What role does prayer play in his family? What books does he have on prayer? How does he teach on prayer? What part would prayer play in the life of this church if he were called here? How would he help to make prayer more meaningful in the lives of other leaders?

Few search committees venture into these types of questions, because many Christians have settled for a private prayer life that is not open to input from fellow leaders or accountability partners. If only we would admit to ourselves that advancing the gospel is really "not by might nor by power but by my spirit," and ask our candidates how they would help us become "a house of prayer," we could open the blinds and shed some light on this important topic. Within the corporate body of Christ, there is probably no other value, apart from the support of evangelism, that we say we believe in but practice so little. Your next leader must be equipped to lead your congregation into a deeper life of prayer.

Word of God: Are the realities of God's Word flowing from his life in ways that demonstrate biblical freedom, rather than legalistic tension? Does the candidate have a steady track record of saturation in the Word and an ability to interpret the winds of culture according to the plumb line of Scripture? Is there integrity of study and personal application of the Word, or is the Bible treated simply as a source for another message outline?

Unfortunately, many seminary graduates have studied so many theories about the authors of Scripture that they have dulled their own convictions about the power of the Holy Spirit to burn God's Word into their hearts. Like the disciples on the Emmaus Road in Luke 24, a pastoral candidate ought to be able to communicate how his heart "burned within him" as he read, studied, prayed over, and obeyed God's Word during the past month. What Scriptures have "leapt off the page" and illuminated his heart and mind recently? What promises have he and his wife written down that they are waiting on God to fulfill? What scriptural insight or guidance has God given him about your church? It is worth the effort for your leaders and committee members to determine how a candidate delights in the Word of the Lord. If a passion for the Word is a prerequisite for any successful candidate, you might never have to listen to another person say as they leave your church, "I'm not being fed here."

3. Check References Thoroughly

Our research shows that a typical search committee in a church or ministry organization moves too quickly to make a decision based on what they "see" on paper or what they "feel" from an interview. Once a primary candidate has been identified, search committees often view the process of reference checking as a "token" requirement to be finished as soon as possible. Glossing over the reference process can be a disastrous mistake.

Robert W. Dingman suggests several reasons why we fall into this trap:

1. Christians are inclined to believe the best about other people—especially spiritual leaders.
2. The search committee and the candidate both put their best foot forward and tend to conceal their flaws and limitations.
3. Good reference checking takes time, courage, and some skill.
4. Search committee members often place too much confidence in their ability to "read people" or to get spiritual "impressions" about the candidates.[4]

For those who are still not convinced of the importance of checking references carefully, allow me to elaborate a bit further on each of Robert Dingman's points:

1. *We have produced a culture of gullibility within the church.* Over the past twenty-four years, I have served on the staff of six churches. None of them asked me penetrating questions in the interviewing process. Only one had a senior pastor who asked his staff questions about their family lives, prayer practices, and personal lives as a regular part of a healthy accountability system. With the emergence of men's movements in our churches, such as Promise Keepers, more of our lay leaders are seeking healthy support, encouragement, and accountability in their relationships. Despite the abuses of the past—such as the Shepherding Movement, which took accountability into toxic levels—it is time for a higher level of peer accountability among church staff members. Staff meetings that focus primarily on scheduling and reporting must be replaced by agendas that prioritize prayer and honest sharing of needs and issues. Let's keep first things first!

Recently, on his own initiative, a youth pastor in a multi-pastor church was able to confess a serious problem with pornography to the other staff members. His colleagues did two commendable things. First, they initiated a restoration process within the church to bring deliverance and healing over the long term. Second, they stepped up the accountability procedures in their own meetings by initiating a series of questions for each other that dealt with "personal" issues in each other's lives. Practicing accountability is not a sign of weakness; it is a sign of wisdom.

Most church leaders consider it inappropriate to ask each other probing questions, and too many search committees make the same mistake in the interview process.

---

2. *Someone must initiate transparency and vulnerability so we can "get everything on the table."* The story of Pastor Steve, mentioned in the introduction, had a good ending. After he and I spoke, Steve decided to take a risk with the search committee and shared with them his weaknesses and ministry failures in past churches. To his amazement, his honesty sparked a spirit of confession among the search committee, which led to a four-hour meeting with tears, repentance, and prayer for their

own failures in church leadership in the past. From that point forward, the level of openness in the process changed dramatically and both the committee and Steve were able to confirm their call together.

Far too often during the search process, churches and leadership candidates seem to follow the Old Testament example of Moses, who put on the veil to hide the fading glory (see 2 Cor. 3:13ff.). We forget that in Christ we have the New Testament freedom to "take off the veil" and deal honestly and lovingly with each other. Just think how much disappointment could be avoided by not creating an illusion during the candidating process of who we really are. Let's be honest with one another and start walking in the light together!

3. *Recruit someone on your committee who will have the courage to ask probing questions, and who has the time and skill to follow up on all references.* Not everyone has the grace to handle these delicate assignments, but it is important that your search committee find someone who is gifted for these important tasks, even if you have to go outside the committee. All references should be checked in person or by phone, because written references are usually carefully crafted to accentuate the positive and may gloss over or ignore significant negative factors.

Because an increasing number of Christian leaders have left positions when a serious problem from the past became known, an opportunity must be given for candidates either to "come clean" or "come away" from the search process. Robert Dingman tells the story of the role he played on one search committee when he left this unusual note in the hotel room of a visiting candidate:

> Friend, if you have anything in your background that has the potential to blow up you and this ministry if it were revealed, I'm sure you don't want to discuss it with me. If by chance this is your situation, I implore you to use any reason you find convenient to withdraw from further consideration.[5]

The next day, when he went to the hotel to pick the candidate up for a search committee meeting, Dingman read the note left for him by the candidate, which said that he needed to discipline a part of his life before he could consider taking on this leadership role.

References should be sought from those who have been in authority over the candidate, those who have been peers, and those who have been subordinates. All of these people should be assured of the absolute confidentiality of their information and that their reference is only one of several you are contacting. See appendix 6 for a sample of a reference check form.

4. *Committee members should avoid "Thus saith the Lord" proclamations to one another.* Spiritual hunches, impressions, or prophetic utterances not only can minimize the perceived need for thorough reference checking, but also they can undermine or sidetrack thorough discussion, reflection, and prayer. Remember, the work of the committee is a group process of confirming God's leading, not a platform for an individual to declare definitively to the group how God is leading. A good ground rule for committee members is not to preface their words with "The Lord says . . . ," because this can damage the unity of the committee so vital to its work. If the Lord has indeed spoken, the group process will confirm it. Once the committee has referred a candidate for approval, church leaders or the corporate body may confirm the work of the committee by means of a prophetic word, if appropriate to that church.

Within the context of the search committee, the misuse of authoritative pronouncements to speak people into positions of authority can be seen as controlling. Unless a search committee is composed solely of church elders, it has no governmental authority, only recommending authority. Leave the promotion and position of church staff to those who have governmental responsibility.

Summary

Integrity—that is, wholeness, soundness, and trustworthiness in character—is what most congregations are looking for in a leader's actions and what they are listening for between the lines of all the carefully prepared messages and public statements he makes. True integrity is revealed under pressure and often can best be seen in the ways a person treats those closest to him when no one is watching. A careful reference-checking process can uncover the truth of a candidate's character in ways that the rest of the interviewing process cannot.

Many pastors in transition and younger pastoral candidates have reported their disappointment in the interview process when character issues are never discussed. It is time for search committees to step up to the plate on this issue and put first things first. Avoiding a candid discussion about character and integrity reflects poorly on the integrity of the search process itself.

CHAPTER 7

RELATIONSHIPS

Identifying the Candidate's People Skills

In an article titled "First-Class Christians, Second-Class Citizens," noted Christian financial advisor Larry Burkett makes the following observations about leadership:

> My friend runs a company with about three thousand employees. He says he wants to relax after retirement and lead a church. . . . I told him that leading a church will ruin his retirement, because the church demands a higher and more complex form of leadership than business does.
>
> The business leader has a clearly defined playing field and enormous leverage with the employees. The leader delivers a product or service through paid staff who either get it done or get replaced. Church leadership is the redeeming and rebuilding of human lives not . . . building widgets or services.
>
> I've read books about Napoleon, de Gaulle, Eisenhower, MacArthur, Patton—all the great military leaders. I don't want to minimize their capabilities or the courage it takes to charge a hill in time of battle, but I've wondered what it would be like for some of those leaders to have to work it out with deacons before they charged up a hill? How well would they do if they had to subject their plans to a vote involving the very people that they're going to

lead up the hill? How would the whole military system work if you took away the leadership leverage of the court-martial?

Anyone could build a church with that kind of leverage! "Teach a Sunday school class or go to the brig." "You call that an offering? Give me fifty push-ups right now." That's leverage!

In the final analysis, we have little or no leverage, no real power over anybody we lead. . . . To mobilize an utterly volunteer organization requires the highest kind of leadership.[1]

Conflicts: Overcoming the "Fight or Flight" Syndrome

Most of us respond to conflict with predictable patterns that have worked for us over the years, especially when the conflict centers on us. If our initial response does not resolve the problem or reduce the escalating tension, we often resort to a backup behavior, which may land us in trouble. Because our secondary response is drawn out under duress, it might manifest itself in a leadership style that is uncharacteristic for us and bring about a confused reaction from others, who thought they knew us better than that. When we swing like a pendulum from avoiding conflict to suddenly engaging in conflict, in the blink of an eye we might appear to change from being Caspar Milquetoast to somewhere between Ghengis Khan and Attila the Hun.

Asking probing questions about a candidate's conflict-resolution style can bring patterns to the surface that the candidate himself may not be aware of. When a search committee asked a prospective pastor named Dave to prepare a brief overview of his history of personal conflicts in the ministry, even Dave was surprised by what he found. When he analyzed his six most difficult conflicts, he discovered the same tendency in each one. He would ignore the problem as long as he could, but when the tension became too great for him to manage, he would "come out like a roaring lion" to "put them in their place" as he described it. The classic "fight or flight" syndrome usually ignores several creative options available for constructively dealing with conflict. Recognizing his tendency to swing from avoidance to attack mode, Dave was able to give the committee an honest assessment of his style. The committee, in turn, had the opportunity to discuss with Dave some potential church tensions and project how he might work with the leadership team to avoid polarizing the congregation. Dave left the meeting with new hope. He felt that he had finally met the people who could work with him in this undeveloped area of his life.

Sadly, conflict theology and conflict methodology are two of the least emphasized topics in our Bible schools and seminaries, yet the inability to resolve conflict is the number one reason cited in exit interviews for prematurely leaving a ministry position. Intra-staff conflict has become a common land mine in the church at large, wounding many of our best emerging leaders. Research from hundreds of pastors and denominational leaders, and feedback from several clergy retreat centers confirms that more staff relationships are maimed and handicapped by unhealthy conflict-resolution practices than by anything else in Satan's arsenal.

To evaluate the maturity level of conflict-resolution skills in your potential leaders, ask them to identify the value they place on allowing healthy conflict. Do they give permission for healthy conflict interactions within the church, just as we would expect to see in a healthy marriage relationship? "Giving permission" means not snuffing out every spark of disagreement between staff or lay leaders. Overemphasis on preserving unity may come across to the staff as an enforced uniformity, which over time will close down meaningful discussion and stifle creativity. Leaders should be able to disagree agreeably with each other without being made to feel they are "sowing seeds of discord" or "touching God's anointed."

Leaders should also provide protection for individuals or groups in conflict by not allowing disrespectful comments, angry outbursts, or inappropriate language. A leader's integrity is primarily measured by how he treats people when he is under great pressure. In the heat and smoke of conflict, the people of God must know that their leaders will protect them—sometimes even from the leaders themselves.

The heated debate recorded in Acts 15, the most important chapter on resolving conflict in the early church, shows how the delicate issue of Gentile circumcision was handled under apostolic protection. Unfortunately, many leaders in the church today learned their patterns for conflict resolution not from the example of Scripture but from highly emotional and unprotected conflict exchanges in their dysfunctional families of origin and other relationships.

In addition to modeling permission and protection, a skillful leader will also empower subordinates or others with weaker communication skills to adequately express their own points of view. This skill, based on the Philippians 2 model of serving others rather than wielding positional power, could be called the skill of "potency."

> Your attitude should be the same as that of Christ Jesus: Who, being in very nature God, did not consider equality with God something to be grasped, but made himself nothing, taking the very nature of a servant, being made in human likeness. (Philippians 2:5–7 NIV)

The key to establishing healthy communication patterns, handling conflict in its early stages—before it gains a foothold and begins to fester—and avoiding the pitfalls of misunderstanding and unnecessary pain, is to bathe every relationship in the healing balm of prayer. Healthy communication flows out of healthy prayer for one another. Regular prayer and repentance for wrong assumptions, defensiveness, misunderstandings about roles and responsibilities, failure to be open with one another, unwillingness to stand in another's shoes, or improper exercise of positional power will create a climate of corporate integrity. Without the renewal and transparency among our leaders that springs from authentic prayer, we will relate to one another more like "peace takers" than peacemakers.

E. Stanley Jones, missionary to India, established a weekly "session of the open heart" with his staff and workers. Any tensions were brought out in an open and loving environment. It was understood that failure to disclose and resolve conflict would wound the body of Christ. Healthy communication kept Jones and his team fighting the real enemy rather than one another. Good leaders practice good listening, careful communication, and diligent prayer, which in turn creates an atmosphere that defuses conflict before it develops into a blowout.

Criticism: "Can You Drink the Cup I Am About to Drink? You Will Drink the Cup."

Every leader has suffered in ways that only another leader can understand. All of us have stories to tell of unjustified criticism, wrong readings of our motives, carnal injustice, and outright demonic attacks. The real issue, however, is how we have processed these incidents. Are we better or bitter as a result?

I have determined never to hire someone without asking him to describe a time of brokenness in his life, especially as it pertains to relationships with others in the work of the ministry. If his description is laced with bitterness, anger, or resentment, then I know he has yet to finish his personal walk with the Good Shepherd through this valley. Until he learns how to deal with brokenness and redemption in his own relationships, he is not fit to lead others effectively.

One way to discern how well a leadership candidate has processed his brokenness is to ask him to describe any experiences of "shattered dreams." Like Joseph in Genesis 37, who was treated unjustly and cast into a pit and later into a prison, a person's ability to lead is determined by how well he handles traumatic times. Joseph's example of showing mercy to his brothers was evidence of his own healing when he said, "You meant it for evil, but God meant it for good." Ask your ministry candidates to describe how God used "pit" and "prison" times in their development.

The mark of a broken leader is that he or she has a much deeper gratitude for the mercy and grace of our Lord. Unless we have wrestled with God in our own disappointment and come out limping, we are not broken. And it is only through authentic brokenness that we will be able to channel God's mercy and grace to our colleagues, coworkers, and congregations when they disappoint us or let us down. In our own un-broken strength, we are more apt to "wash our hands" of people we deem unfit or who don't measure up to their calling. This hardness of heart leads to disaster in the ministry. We must unmask our own stub-born self-will and deal with it. Genuine brokenness is the only posture that prepares us adequately for the spiritual battles we face.

Mentoring: "Imitate Me As I Imitate Christ"

A mentor is someone who has played a formative role in the life of a candidate, either directly or indirectly. Ask each leadership candidate to name other contemporary leaders he looks up to—whose footsteps he would like to follow—and why. Ask him which authors have "mentored" him, and how his life is different as a result.

Ask your prospective leader to tell you about those who have mentored him directly. What is it about the lives and ministries of these mentors that the candidate finds compelling? How and why did each mentor influence the candidate? Have any of these mentors been peers in the ministry?

Though many of today's baby boomer leaders report a significant absence of intentional mentoring in their lives, all of them recognize the crying need to restore this biblically based relational model of leadership development in the church. Younger church members are hungering for mentoring relationships, and most congregations have plenty of resources available among the "old guard." Ask incoming leaders how amenable they are to mentoring others and what experience they have in developing this skill.

Many smaller churches expect their pastor or leaders to spend their time equally among all the members. The idea of spending special time discipling or mentoring others may appear to be showing favoritism. Any leader must be prepared to develop the Ephesians 4 "equipping mandate" as a core value in the church family and exercise wisdom in establishing initial mentoring relationships, until the congregation has assimilated this player-coach model of ministry leadership.

Perspective Power: "Seeing What God Is Doing"

Research has shown that one of the key reasons leaders don't "finish well," even if they start well, is that they lose perspective. Not finishing well, in the context of this book, refers to ending a ministry tenure prematurely or conducting an unhealthy transition to another ministry. "Losing perspective" can be defined as the inability to see what God is doing in the midst of difficult circumstances. Many times it is the counsel of our mentors during this confusion that helps us interpret where God is and what He is doing. That is why we never outgrow our need for mentors to speak truth into our lives. Other times a leader must "encourage himself in the Lord" as David did during one of the most turbulent times in his leadership. Too many church leaders lose perspective and don't know how to regain it. Ask your potential leader if he has any understanding of this dangerous minefield of discouragement.

The prophet Habakkuk was one leader who almost detonated a land mine in his ministry. In chapter 1 of the book of Habakkuk, the prophet loses perspective and complains to God about the injustice and violence of his day (vv. 2–4). He sounds like a modern ministry leader who is about to switch careers, or at least seek a call somewhere else. In chapter 2, he regains his perspective with the revelation that "the righteous will live by his faith" (v. 4 NIV). This verse, quoted by the apostle Paul in the book of Romans, later changed Martin Luther's perspective, which in turn dramatically impacted Europe through the Protestant Reformation. In chapter 3, Habakkuk continues on to "finish well" in the ministry with a restored attitude of faith and rejoicing that comes from a renewed perspective (vv. 17–19).

Every leader needs an anointing of "perspective power." The best way I have found for a leader to gain proper perspective is by completing the developmental time line described in appendix 7. Using selected exercises from J. Robert Clinton's *The Making of a Leader,* the pastor or leader charts out his ministry development to get a clear picture of how God has dealt with him in the past (perspective) and to see how God has used significant others (mentors) to help him move from one phase to the next.[2] I have given this assignment to more than one hundred pastors who have taken my Doctor of Ministry course, and 90 percent of them have said it was the most significant assignment in helping them establish and maintain a proper perspective. I strongly recommend that your search committee ask every serious candidate to do this assignment.

Leadership and People Skills

Looking for the next leader in a church or ministry organization is something like prospecting for gold; the traces we are digging for will help us determine if there is a mother lode of ore under the surface! When evaluating a candidate, look for the following evidences of a "leadership vein":

Positiveness: The ability to work with others and see people and situations in a positive way can make the same difference as pouring gasoline instead of water on a bonfire. A positive outlook can change the working climate of a ministry organization from arctic to tropical. One of the most effective administrators that my seminary recently hired was given a standard farewell party from his colleagues in another department of our university before taking his new position with us. Those of us who attended were convinced of our right choice when we heard the numerous moving testimonies of this man's treatment of employees in stressful situations. The legacy of his leadership was that, over the years, his positive attitude had changed the climate of his workplace.

Follow-through: Unfortunately, in many churches and ministries, letting your "Yes" be "Yes" and your "No" be "No" has become the exception rather than the rule. A consistent track record of getting the job done completely and in a timely manner is a mark of character as well as of skill. It represents a willingness to do what is required regardless of personal moods, circumstances, or inconveniences. One of the references I called a few years ago about a pastoral candidate put it this way: "Brother Jack does what he says he is going to do."

Self-discipline: In the potentially explosive climate of pursuing a ministry, a potential leader must consistently demonstrate self-discipline in two key areas: time and emotions. The discipline of not allowing another's actions to dictate one's responses is a leadership quality cast from pure gold. By taking full responsibility for his own emotional state while dealing with turbulent feelings in others, the self-disciplined leader has a freedom to love people who are being unlovable.

The discipline of effective time management challenges every leader, especially in the areas of overwork and underwork. Studies of creativity have shown that consistent excellence does not come from tired people! Overwork was not a mark of Jesus' ministry. He did no more and no less than what the Father showed Him and told Him each and every day.

Underwork usually comes from a habit of procrastination, which can cause us to miss the *kairos* of God—the significant moment in time that God wants to do something through us. Redeeming the time has a lot to do with not being asleep during the harvest, and being "in season" with the timing of God. Procrastinators who get caught up in the *chronos*—the ticking away of hours, days, and months—don't know what time it is in the kingdom and usually miss the *kairos*.

Sometimes consistent procrastination is a symptom of unresolved rebellion in the life of a leader. Somewhere along the line he has opted for procrastination as a way of saying "No!" to responsibilities. Discerning this tendency in a candidate will help the search committee avoid the potential people problems that arise from this behavior.

Communication Skills: During one pastoral search that I observed, several church members approached the elders after meeting a potential leader at a church picnic and said, "It seems that he gives himself 100 percent to the other person when he is conversing. I felt as if I was the most important person in the world during our conversation." Good eye contact, a warm smile, and the ability to focus on the other person are learned skills that reveal the heart of a leader for others and his desire to grow in effectiveness. Look for leaders who fulfill the John 10:3 mandate to first "call the sheep by name" before they attempt to "lead them out."

Three qualities of effective ministry communication with individuals are *identification, edification,* and *impartation.* When Scripture declares that "the Word became flesh and dwelt among us" (John 1:14 NKJV), it describes the key principle of *identification* with those to whom we are speaking and ministering. Jesus intentionally left His own frame of reference, which was the throne of God, and entered into the paradigm and mind-set of those to whom He was sent to communicate the message of salvation (see Phil. 2:5–7).

Potential leaders must demonstrate by their track record and in the interview process that they can set aside their academic "ivory tower" thinking or their "churchianity subculture" vocabulary to identify with real people in the real world. Would-be leaders who cannot connect with teens or young adults, at least on a one-to-one basis, will have a difficult time leading the church into the twenty-first century. Identification takes a continual, proactive effort by a leader to break out of one's comfort zone.

Effective communication skills are also demonstrated in the way a leader practices *edification*. Modeled after the description of Jesus in Hebrews 4:15 ("For we do not have a High Priest who cannot sympathize with our weaknesses . . ."), edification is the ability to express empathy with a troubled person's concerns and circumstances. Far from approaching others from behind a contrived professional veneer, edification springs from an attitude of genuineness described by Paul in Philippians 2:20. It also includes the emotional warmth modeled by the apostle when he describes himself as "kind and tenderhearted" toward his followers. The end result of edification is that others feel prized, special, and strengthened by their interactions with the leader. Edification is a communication skill that can cover a multitude of other, underdeveloped leadership traits.

The third communication skill, *impartation*, refers to a leader's ability to transmit to others the power of "the blessing" described by John Trent and Gary Smalley in their excellent book by the same title.[3] When Isaac laid his hands on Jacob, he transferred something to his son that impacted generations after him. Though often misunderstood in the modern church, the blessing, as described by Smalley and Trent, involves speaking words that encourage a sense of "high value" (see Gen. 27:27–29) and promote the expectation of a "hopeful future" (see Gen. 3:15; Rom. 15:14). The ability or tendency to impart a blessing is more than just a trait of a particular personality. It is a key ingredient of a leader's calling according to apostolic exhortation (1 Peter 3:9).

Questions for Discussion

1. How has your potential leader dealt with conflict and criticism in the past? Is there a consistent record of integrity and maturity in this critical area of leadership?

2. How has your potential leader processed hard times in the past, especially times of disappointment and disillusionment? Is there

evidence of a healthy spiritual brokenness or is there evidence of a wounded spiritual bitterness?

3. What roles are mentors playing in the life of your potential leader? Is there evidence of an ability to develop healthy relationships that release people into the purposes that God has for them?

4. Which leadership and people skills described in this chapter does your potential leader demonstrate? Is there evidence of good principles of time management? How well has the leader done in the areas of identification, edification, and impartation?

See appendix 8 for an extensive list of additional questions that your search committee can customize for use in the candidate interview process.

PART THREE

MODELS AND METHODS FOR THE CANDIDATE

CHAPTER 8

DANGEROUS DATING DELUSIONS

"He was the senior pastor who recommended that the church hire me. It was only six months later that I discovered in him the dangerous combination of insecurity, poor communication, and a need for control. We never had regular staff meetings in the two years I was there. The only time I met with him was when he thought I had done something wrong. He would publicly humiliate me from the pulpit. Instead of telling me he didn't want me to have access to a certain room or area that I had previously been given access to, he'd change the lock. I never knew when he was changing his mind, or why. I cried every night those first eighteen months.

"I guess the saddest part of this saga is that I felt that this was my 'cross to bear.' I should have seen from the beginning that this pastor had problems. I was his first female staff person and he seemed to become intimidated by me. After I left, the integrity crisis came out. The pastor collapsed morally, and the church has not yet recovered."

The Cinderella Syndrome

Webster's New World Dictionary defines *romance* as "a fictitious tale of wonderful and extraordinary events, characterized by much imagination and idealization; without basis in fact; an exaggeration or falsehood." In other words, romance is fed more by fantasy than reality, which is why many couples in courtship have a hard time seeing anything but perfection in each other, despite evidence to the contrary. In dating relationships and pastoral/staff searches, we can get so caught up in looking for our Prince Charming or Cinderella that we begin to burden ourselves with unrealistic expectations—sometimes called the "Cinderella syndrome."

I have seen too many couples who have missed some rather obvious character flaws in each other because they were blinded by life pressures or the proverbial "biological clock." The same dynamic can complicate a leadership candidate's ability to clearly confirm his or her call to a particular ministry.

The Halo Effect

When a candidate feels a compelling need to "get a job," rebound from a bad experience, justify the years spent in Bible school or seminary, or receive affirmation of his or her significance, it can lead to an illusion—much like a desert mirage—called the "halo effect." One seasoned clergy deployment professional explains it this way:

> The halo effect is the tendency to see any church as you want it to be, either in terms of being better than it really is, or in terms of possessing the particular characteristics you are looking for.[1]

The problem with the halo effect is that its intensity seems to increase in direct proportion to our need to receive a new call. If we're not careful, we can easily make the same mistake repeated every year by thousands of disillusioned married couples in our country when one or both of the partners mistakenly thinks they can change the other to match whatever their idealized "Ken and Barbie" image is of their mate. If you think that by receiving a "call" you will be able to transform a church into your ideal ministry opportunity, you may be no more successful than the divorced couples who fill the pews every Sunday.

As a candidate, you should ask yourself, "If I am called, what will I wish I had known about the church six months from now?" Also, you would be wise to question clergy friends individually or gather a group of them together before your interview and ask them to answer the following question: "What would you have liked to have known about the churches you pastored before you accepted the call?" Use their combined experience and wisdom, along with creative brainstorming, to help you formulate questions to ask the search committee.

Don't be blinded by the halo effect. Do your best to see the prospective church as it is, not as you want it to be. Remember, the church without the halo is the one you will be getting. Reality will be somewhere between the church you envision in your heart of hearts and the one that calls you. Even if the church without the halo is worse than you initially perceived, God may still have led you there to serve His purpose. Depending on your gifting, God may be calling you to open your eyes and "count the cost" of serving in a specific ministry.

The "Falling-in-Love" Expectation

By drawing a parallel between the matching of a potential leader with a church and the courtship process leading to marriage, we put ourselves in deep water. Our post-Christian Western culture offers no successful formula for finding a marriage partner. Through the steps of becoming acquainted, dating, going steady, becoming engaged, and exchanging the wedding vows, our society gives us no clear guidelines to ensure we're making the right match for a whole lifetime. Even godly parents can disagree about the best marital matching process for their children.

Those cultures that practice some version of arranged marriages, where the parents find "a suitable partner" for their children, claim that their success rate for good matches is better than those societies that follow the "falling-in-love" method. In fact, my Asian friends claim more biblical support for arranged marriages. If we can apply this principle to the task of matching leaders with ministries, it would seem that churches that require a higher organizational authority (such as a bishop, district pastor, or denominational leaders) to initiate or make a leadership placement should have the most "successful" churches. Although this correlation does not necessarily hold true, there is a movement today among emerging independent churches for departing pastors to choose their successors. In chapter 11, we will discuss a ministry model for "raising up the next generation" that has proven successful.

Throughout the process of seeking ministry opportunities, interviewing, and considering a call, the role of your spouse must not be minimized. Both husband and wife must experience each stage of the procedure to help each other counteract the halo effect or the "falling-in-love" expectation. Failing to include your spouse at each step will greatly increase your chances of echoing this painful story:

> During the two years we were at the church, she never said, "I told you so!" but she might well have. It had happened almost exactly as she had feared. I should have known that my life partner ought to be the one who knew me best. I should have listened more intently to her caring instincts. She, of all people, knew my strengths and weaknesses, and felt from the beginning that this "new marriage" might be a mismatch. . . .[2]

Shotgun Weddings: Need-Driven vs. Spirit-Led

The "Eager-Beaver" Candidate

Our research has shown that the hardest candidates to evaluate by a search committee are those who are under great pressure to leave their present ministries, or those who are wandering in the no-man's-land of unemployment. Difficult circumstances tempt a candidate to try to match himself to what the search committee is looking for rather than just being himself. Similar to the desperation exhibited by a jilted lover or a new divorcé who makes another poor choice "on the rebound," a candidate under pressure does not see the church or himself in an objective light. He has a difficult time clarifying his core values and seems all too ready to exaggerate any strengths that he discovers the search committee is looking to find.

Search committees have a reputation for slow turnaround times in communicating with possible candidates. By contrast, the Eager Beaver may seem to put on a "full-court press" in his efforts to speed up the process. Though some committee members may initially interpret this demonstration of diligence and enthusiasm as evidence of a "call" in the candidate's heart, his sense of urgency may actually reveal a lack of trust in God's sovereignty and timing. Impatience with the process may be a red flag to both the candidate and the committee that there are issues of the heart and the wallet that need to be addressed.

The "Special-Needs" Candidate

The truth of the candidating process is that most of us get turned down more often than we are selected. Rejection doesn't feel good no matter how we try to spiritualize it, but repeated rejection or delay can bump even the best of us into the "special needs" bin. Here's a typical scenario:

After a series of "no calls" from different churches, the candidate finds what he believes is the right opportunity. A search committee member calls and requests permission for the candidate's name to be considered. He says "yes"—and then nothing happens. Several weeks pass. A reference person calls saying the search committee seems interested—and then nothing happens. A month goes by. Eventually he hears that he is one of several candidates being considered—and then nothing happens. Now it begins to seem like the church is deliberately stalling. The candidate waits impatiently by the phone for the next stage in the process. This is a dangerous time when he will be tempted to force a premature decision or in some way sabotage the process.

A subtle danger creeps into the candidating process after several rejections. A growing sense of weariness and loss of hope can lead to a time of depression and confusion regarding our sense of identity and call to the ministry. We are tempted to think we are looking for a job instead of trying to discern the right place to invest ourselves in God's service. Times of waiting are good opportunities to fine-tune our spiritual disciplines and refresh our spiritual nourishment. A season of saturation in the Psalms in a modern translation, such as *The Message* by Eugene Peterson, can help us identify and express negative emotions before they take our thoughts into captivity. We may discover that a "no" call may be an affirmation to stay where we are and deal with some issues we've been unwilling to face until now.

Another helpful exercise to build "persevering power" during these times is to consider the eight distinct events, identified by Loren Mead, that a congregation experiences between one pastor and the next:

1. *Termination:* Many times members of the congregation feel "terminated" by the pastor when he announces his resignation. Hurt feelings, disappointment, and bitterness are similar to some of the dynamics in a divorce. Unfortunately, the departing pastor often does not have a strategy for helping his grieving congregation through this season of change.
2. *Direction Finding:* With the pastor's departure comes a heightened

sense of anxiety about the procedures to follow in seeking a replacement. If most of the leadership connections or denominational executive relationships were formed by the pastor, there may be few others in the congregation who know whom to call or whom to trust for advice. With so much to learn in such a short time, some may feel overwhelmed. With decisions on interim pastors, consultants, search committees, and budgets, it takes time to sort out the church's priorities and make wise decisions.

3. *Self-Study:* This evaluation process is critical for ensuring the right match between the church and its new leader. The strength and validity of the church profile depends on the abilities and commitment of those who put it together. Although profiling the church will consume most of the search committee's time, even the best profile is only "a working document, the product of a flawed group of people trying to say something they can live with about themselves."[3]

4. *Search:* Search committees typically underestimate the number of people who will inquire about their vacancy—sometimes fifty or more in a three-week period. The process may grind to a halt while the committee tries to figure out a workable system to manage all of the incoming data. Any businesspeople on the committee may begin to panic when they realize how their own businesses would falter if they were as unprepared as the committee in giving timely responses to these inquiries.

5. *Decision and Negotiation:* Most churches have little experience in reaching a clear decision about calling a pastor. The process of formalizing the relationship varies from one congregation to another, and may include contracts, covenants, or letters of agreement. This critical step usually happens much later than anticipated.[4]

The "Smother Brother" Candidate

Sometimes in premarital courtship, we try to distinguish ourselves by paying special attention to the little things in a relationship: the special flowers, the little notes, the perfectly arranged evening. But if we never stop to give the other person some "breathing space" to process what is happening in the relationship, he or she may soon feel smothered by our actions.

When these same kinds of characteristics show up in the leadership selection process—the detailed résumé; well-organized documentation of materials; precise answers to every inquiry by phone, mail, or in person; weekly follow-up calls from the candidate—the committee would be wise to look behind the impressive display to discern the candidate's motives. This type of behavior may mask a tendency toward control—a trait that has made many a spouse or new pastor quite difficult to live with.

The "Messiah Complex" Candidate

Perfectionism—and its cousin, performance orientation—can lead to early burnout and a short pastoral tenure. Sometimes referred to as the messiah complex, it causes a pastor to carry too much of the burden for the emotional and spiritual health of the congregation. There is no rest until every detail is covered. All his energy is focused on doing everything to perfection, which he may try to justify by referring to the biblical mandate to have a "spirit of excellence."

One reliable indicator of perfectionism or performance orientation is how well a candidate responds to criticism. Typically, a perfectionist will overreact or be hypersensitive to criticism and may take everything personally. Constructive criticism of a sermon by a healthy parishioner may send a perfectionist pastor into a tailspin of self-reproach. He regards every sermon as either a home run or a strikeout. There is no in-between. Perfectionists are all-or-nothing kinds of people. They don't last long in healthy churches.

There is a subtle temptation in ministry leadership to move from grace-based to performance-based ministry. The symptoms include equating our personal worth with our accomplishments, craving the praise of people, finding our identity in what we alone can do, and living in a constant mode of drivenness without a clue about how to enter into God's rest on a regular basis. The end result of this "works righteousness" is that we take ownership of the ministry based on an unhealthy pride in what we do, have our own agenda that refuses to seek godly counsel, operate by our own set of "rules," and become unwilling to lay a part of or all of the ministry down for a season as necessary. Messiah complex leaders are not healthy leaders. Be sure that your search committee knows what a healthy leader looks like before you base your decision on someone's track record of accomplishments.

Research Summaries

Our research discovered four key reasons why ministry candidates misplace themselves in new positions:

1. *Unrealistic Assessment of Their Gifts* (24%). New graduates going into ministry often display immaturity and ignorance as they try to move from the ideals of the classroom to the realities of a ministerial position that requires maturity and gifts they may not yet possess. This may be due to a lack of reflection on their strengths and weaknesses. It may also be due to a lack of practical experience in the area in which they wish to minister.
2. *Unrealistic Assessment of the Church* (22%). This is due in part to the candidate's inability or unwillingness to properly assess the organization to which he or she is seeking a call. It may also be due to the failure of the church to clearly define its values, expectations, history, and mission.
3. *Unrealistic Assessment of Their Call* (22%). Instead of seeking God's will, candidates too often are influenced by family and friends. Many new candidates are unclear about what God is calling them to do, and they may accept unsuitable positions. They have not done a sufficient spiritual assessment to sense where the Spirit of God is moving in their lives.
4. *Selfish Motivations* (20%). The following motivations seemed to appear in equal numbers in both new candidates and experienced ones seeking a new position.
    a. *Tired of present position.* Many will seek new positions simply because they are tired of their present ministry problems and want to get away to "greener pastures."
    b. *Desire for more salary/benefits.* These candidates approach a new ministry position from the same perspective as their neighbors in secular work.
    c. *Stepping-stone positions.* Some candidates choose positions based on their personal ambitions and view new opportunities in terms of prestige or prominence.

On behalf of the wounded pastors and staff members, and the church committees that called them, we must work harder to avoid ministry mismatches. Churches and candidates alike can strive to eliminate the pitfalls that have resulted in disillusionment for too many leaders. It begins with a healthier way of relating to one another in the matching process. There's no better time to start than now, when we are seeking the kind of people who can lead us into the twenty-first century.

CHAPTER 9

KNOW THYSELF
Lust or Love?

"I just left my first full-time ministry position after two-and-a-half years as a youth pastor in a conservative church. I almost died there. The major problem was a total lack of any type of relationship with the senior pastor. The staff spent only thirty minutes per week together for planning, nothing else. We never, absolutely never, prayed together.

"In His providence, God moved me to my current position. After four months, I know I am in the right place. Looking back, I can see that I learned a lot from my ordeal. I'm wondering if those two years were a preparation for this? Could my 'now' only have come as a result of my discouraging and difficult 'then'? Could it be that God is still in the redemptive business? I know He is."

Self-Assessment Methods

"Am I really in love or is this just my hormones?" "Is this what I want to do or is it what I am expected to do?" "Who am I, anyway?" These classic adolescent thoughts may be questions that many of us haven't asked since our days of pimples and proms. Yet our research has determined that identifying the "real you" and being comfortable expressing who you really are to others is the hinge that swings the gate open to effective ministry matching.

Churches searching for pastors may have difficulty negotiating the treacherous steps to discovering who they really are, and without a strong search committee that has taken the contents of this book to heart, the church may not handle the "courtship process" very well. However, a well-prepared candidate who has done a rigorous self-examination of his own motives can make up for deficiencies from the church's side. The hard work done in the early stages creates hope for the long-term process. But unless you approach each ministry opportunity well prepared, you risk being taken in by hype in the church's promotion of itself.

God's Word tells us that our hearts are deceitful, and this deceit may cause us to focus on the wrong factors when we evaluate a ministry. The prophet Balaam became so fixated on the amount he would be paid for cursing the people of God that he ignored what God had clearly said to him the first time he inquired. In Numbers 22:12, God said, "Do not go with them; you shall not curse the people; for they are blessed" (NASB). When Balak upped the ante (v. 17), Balaam's greed deceived him into inquiring of the Lord again (v. 19). This time, God gave him a different word: "If the men have come to call you, rise up and go with them; . . ."

Balaam was deceived by the idol of money, which caused him to hear according to the carnal desires of his heart. "Everyone of the house of Israel who sets up his idols in his heart . . . I the LORD will answer him who comes, *according to the multitude of his idols*" (Ezek. 14:4 NKJV, italics added).

Before we inquire of God, or go too far down the road of courting a church or ministry, we must tear down the idols of carnal passions or unmet needs and get in touch with our real, God-given heart passions. We must fight the tendency to try to be someone we're not, especially for our first candidating experience. There will always be a temptation to pretend to be just the person we think the committee is looking for. That strategy may work in the "gentile" secular world, but Jesus says, "Not so with you." The best thing we can do for ourselves, our families, and our potential churches is to know who we are and be that person.

Why Am I Considering This Move?

Honesty with ourselves may bring us to realize that we are not going to find fulfillment or job satisfaction in our present situation. If we're experiencing this transition anxiety for the first time, there is a danger of submitting to the condemnation of the adversary, especially when we hear ourselves saying, "It wasn't supposed to be like this!" But if we have some honest friends, we may discover with their help that it is time to move on. Prolonged conflict may have taken its toll. Perhaps we can see that we are underemployed in our present circumstances and our boredom with the culture in our church will kill us if we don't find something to challenge us.

The first question we must ask is foundational: Should we even be in ministry leadership? In *The Power of the Call,* Henry Blackaby and Henry Brandt exhort us to stand freshly before God and His Word to comprehend the clarity of our call and recapture its joy.[1] Whenever we are in the process of being considered by a church to become a pastor, these wise counselors remind us to

1. *Bring our lives before the Lord—as His servants.* To deny ourselves and take up our cross is to have the God-given motivation to help these precious saints come from where the Lord has taken them with another leader to where He wants to take them with us. It is important that we appreciate how God has been working in this church long before our name was considered as a potential leader. If we think that we have to clean house in order to do God's work, we may be cleaning out the work that God has already done.

2. *Pray! Pray! Pray!* Pray for integrity of heart that has no personal agenda, no self-willed schemes, no self-centered goals. As we release our wills to Him, before He has made His will clear, we are able to receive clear assignments that might totally surprise us. Our goal is to join with God in what He is already doing. Therefore, we need to discern what He is about and ask Him whether this is the time that we should join Him in His work. "For it is God who works in you both to *will* and to *do* for His good pleasure" (Phil. 2:13 NKJV, italics added).

If I know that I am motivated or have the "will," how can I know "how" I am motivated? Common tools used by church leaders today are inventories, assessments, and profiles. Used properly in the right balance with prayer and other Spirit-led measures, they help identify a candidate's unique mix of gifts, talents, temperament, and passions. These testing tools serve as "checks and balances" to help you avoid a ministry mismatch.[2]

Temperament Inventories

Our surveys revealed that few evangelical or charismatic/Pentecostal churches use temperament inventories, probably because not many of their pastors were trained to understand the role these tests could play in the matching process. We have already begun to see the value of these instruments in premarital counseling, and perhaps the day is coming when churches and training schools will follow suit. Churches in mainline denominations that have used temperament inventories have discovered the value of these tools for eliciting the distinctive qualities of a potential leader. Because seminaries by and large train students as though they must be competent in all aspects of ministry, many search committees have discovered that most pastoral profiles they receive look alike. A temperament inventory can more clearly show an individual's particular gifts and tendencies.

1. Keirsey Temperament Sorter

This profile is helpful in revealing temperaments using the same categories as the well-known Myers-Briggs Type Indicator (MBTI). The chapter called "Temperament in Leading," in David Keirsey and Marilyn Bates's *Please Understand Me,* explains this instrument in an easily readable fashion.[3] The Keirsey Temperament Sorter is recommended over the MBTI instrument in matching a particular type of person with a particular type of congregation.

2. DiSC Inventory

The DiSC Inventory is used to identify motivations and behavioral tendencies shown by combinations of four basic personality types. Identified by the letters D, i, S, and C, these types are described as

- "D": Dominant, Direct, Demanding, and Decisive
- "i": Inspiring, Influential, Impressing, and Inducing
- "S": Submissive, Steady, Stable, and Security-oriented
- "C": Competent, Compliant, Cautious, and Calculating

This inventory shows how we see ourselves and how others see us. It also reveals our perceptions of "what is expected of us." These insights help to explain why some situations frustrate us and others energize us. It's interesting to note that as specific circumstances in our lives change, the results of this inventory will likely change accordingly. For example, my own DiSC score was notably different when I changed my focus from pastoral care to church planting. An excellent, biblically based book on this topic is *Understanding How Others Misunderstand You,* by Ken Boges and Ron Braund.

Leadership Profiles

The corporate world is flooded with numerous leadership profiles that reveal the characteristics of leaders, the styles of leaders, or the different roles of leaders, either as individuals or in teams. The most helpful to our purposes in ministry matching include the following:

1. Role Preference Inventory

The Role Preference Inventory is based on a model in which all organizations and their related projects fall into one of five phases.[4]

- In the *Design* phase, new and original ideas are welcomed with a premium put on those that are creative and innovative.
- In the *Design Development* phase, the value lies with who can put legs to an idea and bring in healthy structure and organization.
- In the *Development* phase, workable plans are developed for long- and short-term strategies.
- In the *Development Management* phase, plans are refined and tweaked to obtain maximum results.
- In the *Management* phase, things are running smoothly and efficiently and need to be maintained at this quality level.

By identifying your dominant preference within the framework of the stages of an organization, you can understand what kind of "player" you prefer to be: captain, middle captain, or strong player.

In the context of effective ministry matching, immediate benefits come from understanding our role preferences. First, it will help to determine which roles describe what we really want to do, not what we are doing, or what we think others expect of us. Second, we will find personal fulfillment when we are in a position for which we were designed. Third, when we know what positions are the best fit, it's easier to "just say no" to opportunities that may meet our short-term financial needs but result in burnout or premature turnover. Fourth, it will be easier and quicker to determine which positions we should seriously consider.

2. C.A.R.E. Profile

Similar in a lot of ways to the Role Preference Inventory is the C.A.R.E. Profile published by Carlson Learning Company. This instrument is specifically designed to measure one's contribution to the team in the daily environment of pastoral ministry. C.A.R.E. recognizes that individuals tend to take on roles within a team based on different approaches to innovation and teamwork. "Creators" generate concepts and ideas. "Advancers" get excited about ideas from the Creators and are good at developing ways to promote and move these ideas toward implementation. "Refiners" are gifted at challenging concepts and identifying potential flaws and problems in ideas so that implementation may be successful. "Executors" are those who are energized by the implementation of ideas and projects.

3. Situational Leadership

Paul Hersey and Ken Blanchard's Situational Leadership profile examines a leader's adaptability in relation to the maturity level of a follower.[5] This model was developed by examining the amount of direction and support a leader needs to give in assigning a specific task. Maturity level is defined as the degree to which the follower has had successful experiences doing the specific task (for example evangelism or discipleship). The "maturity" of an individual will vary according to experience in each task. As the maturity of the individual or group increases, the leader moves along a continuum from "telling" to "selling" to "participating" to "delegating."

- *Telling:* The leader gives specific, detailed instructions regarding the task.
- *Selling:* The leader engages the follower in two-way communication, giving significant instructions while eliciting support from the follower.
- *Participating:* The leader allows the follower to use his or her own abilities and knowledge while still receiving significant support from the leader.
- *Delegating:* Delegation can be used when the follower is self-motivated and able to complete the task with little direction or support from the leader.

This tool is best used in a group setting to measure the group's maturity level, which in turn provides guidance to the leader on how best to lead the group to the next level. Consequently, it may have its greatest impact on a leader's ability to achieve a longer tenure in a ministry, rather than as a matching instrument. The value to a pastoral candidate lies in determining his ability to choose the appropriate leadership style to adapt to the levels of leadership demanded by a situation.

4. Leadership Practices Inventory (LPI)

The LPI was developed by discovering common practices evident in "extraordinary leadership achievements."[6] This inventory is used to determine where our strengths and weaknesses are in five key areas. The five practices of extraordinary leaders are "challenging," "inspiring," "enabling," "modeling," and "encouraging."

- *Challenging the Process* involves searching for opportunities, experimenting, and taking risks.
- *Inspiring a Shared Vision* involves envisioning the future and enlisting the support of others.
- *Enabling Others to Act* involves fostering collaboration and strengthening others.
- *Modeling the Way* involves setting an example and planning small wins.
- *Encouraging the Heart* involves recognizing contributions and celebrating accomplishments.[7]

The workbook that contains this inventory includes information on analyzing and interpreting scores and has more than 130 suggestions on how to improve and strengthen daily leadership practices. This is a helpful personal growth and assessment tool for all leaders.

Spiritual Gifts Test

Of the numerous spiritual gift tests available, two of the most helpful are described here.

Wagner-Modified Houts Questionnaire

This questionnaire contains 125 questions that assess the twenty-five areas of gifting defined by Peter Wagner in *Your Spiritual Gifts Can Help Your Church Grow.*[8] The questionnaire includes a review of gift definitions and Scripture references but no discussion of application issues.

Spiritual Gifts Profile

The Spiritual Gifts Profile compiled by Mels Carbonell is a broad-stroke assessment based on the seven motivational gifts described in Romans 12.[9] Combined with a DiSC profile, a talent inventory, a conflict-style instrument, and a leadership insights analysis, this profile is a unique tool for pastors and evangelists.

Other Tools

Aubrey Malphurs offers an excellent chapter entitled "The Practice of Assessment" in his book *Pouring New Wine Into Old Wineskins*.[10] Using the example of Nehemiah as a leader and administrator, Malphurs offers research on the specific personality characteristics of effective "revitalization pastors." An interesting comparison is made between the characteristics of paradigm pioneers (change agents) and the life of Nehemiah. Change agents emphasize the following traits: Catalyst (Neh. 2:1–3, 11), Outsider (1:1), Problem Solver (1:3), Visionary (2:17), Motivator (2:17–18), Persuader (2:4–8), Risk Taker (2:1–2, 16–17), Empathizer (1:4, 8–11), Perseverer (4:1–6:14), Planner (2:6–8), Recruiter (2:17–20), Organizer (3:1, 3), Delegator (3ff.).

God's Armor Bearer by Terry Vance is a tool not specifically related to assessment instruments, but it serves transitioning leaders in a unique way.[11] This material addresses the attitudes we must have when we take on a ministry position that will require us to report to someone else.

CHAPTER 10

INTERVIEWING
Getting Past the Mating Rituals

The search committee regrets to report that after reviewing their résumés and references, the following candidates have failed to meet our qualifications:

- *Noah*—He has no converts even after preaching for 120 years. This could indicate a "credibility gap." In addition he may have a drinking problem according to one of his sons.
- *Abram/Abraham*—First of all, why is he using two names? Is one an alias? We've heard that he will stoop to bend the truth when it suits his purposes. And just who is head of his household? His wife was heard laughing when he was talking to God. Perhaps if they would agree to some personal and marriage counseling, we would consider them at another time.
- *Moses*—We were leaning toward Moses but couldn't overlook two of his problems. One is his stuttering and stammering and the other is his tendency to lose his temper once in a while.
- *David*—We certainly were impressed with his talent in writing music and poetry, but we haven't heard whether he can preach. Of course, when we heard of his moral lapse, we knew we couldn't have him as pastor. Maybe later when the church can afford it, he could be considered for a position as minister of music.
- *Solomon*—He seems to spend a lot of time on his writing. The thing that really clinched it for us though was his lavish lifestyle. Add to

that all his dependents and we don't think we could give him the benefits package he would expect.

- *Elijah*—He certainly comes with powerful preaching references! However, we don't think that his sarcasm is appropriate for reaching the unchurched. Besides, he seems to have a tendency toward self-pity.
- *Jeremiah*—What we really need around here is an upbeat preacher, one who can really "edify" us. We feel that Jeremiah would be too depressing for most our members.
- *John the Baptist*—We were impressed with the results he gets when he preaches—but the way he dresses! And how about the way he eats? What if he brought a honey-dipped insect casserole to one of our covered-dish suppers?
- *Matthew*—With his background in finance, instead of theology, he would probably sound more like an accountant. And we don't think our people can handle too many sermons on stewardship.
- *Luke*—Here again is the background issue. He is trained in medicine, not theology. Besides, why would anyone leave such a lucrative position unless he is running from a lawsuit or something?
- *Peter*—We need leadership around here, but not the kind of preacher who carries a sword around and smells like fish most of the time. Maybe we could partially support him later as a missionary down at the docks.
- *Paul*—Yes, he has a great preaching résumé, but how often would he be in our pulpit? He always seems to want to move somewhere else and we don't really have any backups.
- *Jesus*—Jesus is a good storyteller and can clearly attract a crowd. However, he is single and we feel we need a married man for this position.[1]

Putting Yourself on Paper

No doubt there have been major discrepancies between some pastors' résumés and who they are in real life. Nevertheless, a well-written personal profile will demonstrate a "spirit of excellence" and cause a candidate to stand out. The bottom line for any search committee is that they want to see that you have a track record of competence in your current position. In other words, have you made a difference in your present church? Many committees decide up front not to even look at someone who isn't presently involved in a ministry profession.[2]

The main purpose for carefully identifying your unique qualities on your résumé or profile is that you want to receive a call—and you want to receive the *right* call. In his excellent book, *Opening the Clergy Parachute*, Christopher Moore puts it this way:

> Getting a call has to do with presenting yourself and your ministry as effectively as possible. Getting the right call has to do with being selective in deciding which aspects of your ministry you choose to emphasize; even if the end result may narrow the range of possibilities you may encounter.[3]

What you want to achieve in the process of getting things down on paper is to keep the matching as simple, clear, and practical as possible. Simply stated, it means writing your strengths on the left-hand column of a piece of paper and the church's needs and opportunities on the right-hand column. This exercise will help you to determine whether your particular strengths would be used in this church and whether the church's expectations would require competencies that you possess.

The Interview

After your résumé has been accepted, you should receive notice of the first interview. A common mistake that applicants make in preparing for an interview is weighing the church's denominational history too heavily. It is crucial for pastors to know that the culture and geography of a region will have more influence on the beliefs and behaviors of parishioners than the particular denomination of the church to which they belong. Baptists or Presbyterians in North Dakota, for example, will practice their distinctives differently than Baptists or Presbyterians in North Carolina. A North Dakota Presbyterian may be more comfortable in a North Dakota Lutheran church than in a North Carolina Presbyterian church. Whatever the denominational affiliation, or lack thereof, make sure that the discussions emphasize the church's culture at least as much as its denominational connections.

Much has been written on how to conduct a "successful" job interview.[4] The goal of this book is not to help you land a job that might turn into a disappointment for you and your congregation, but to encourage you to confirm a ministry partnership together with the church. The bottom line in the interview is for the candidate and the ministry to mutually explore whether God is calling them into a covenant relationship. Adopting this perspective will make a world of difference.

Our research has revealed that too much emphasis is placed on the controlled environment of the interview. Some candidates make a better first impression than others, even though the others might be more qualified to meet the needs of that particular church. We highly recommend that serious candidates spend at least a "relaxed" weekend with the committee and others in the church to conduct informal discussions without suits and ties and carefully crafted responses.[5] Let's put an end to the "old wineskin" process of having only one major interview and replace it with a more relationship-based approach to confirming God's call between leader and church.

One of Lyle Schaller's techniques that I often share with my graduating students is humorously close to a backroom poker game. Give each search committee member a set of ten to fifteen index cards, on which you have printed the numerous roles of a pastor, such as visitation, preaching, counseling, administration, discipling, and so on. After handing each of the members a "stack of cards," ask them to privately rearrange them into the order of priorities that they believe the new pastor should emphasize. Then, at the same moment, everyone "lays their cards" on the table.

You will discover two things in the process. The first is whether or not the committee is united regarding pastoral priorities. The second is whether your priorities match theirs.

One of my ministry mentors once told me that survey results are only as valuable as the amount of discussion they generate. Because candidates usually put on their résumés only what they think they should or what they think you are looking for, the only way to find out what they really think is to connect in a personal discussion. That is why the interview process is imperative for both the church and the candidate.

In the interview, each side will discover the other's identity by revealing important norms, customs, habits, and past events that were not mentioned in the profiles. Roy Oswald recommends the following historical issues of churches that should be discussed in the interview:

- The congregation's beginnings
- The leaders or "heroes" who are remembered
- "Days of Glory" that are recalled
- Memories of crises and turmoil

- The hopes and dreams accumulated over the years (usually associated with church buildings)
- Families or individuals who were key to this history, some of whom may still be around.[6]

Questions Behind the Questioning

One professional who has helped many pastoral candidates understand how to get to the key issues during the limited time of the interview offers these deeper meanings behind the typically asked questions:

Questions from the Church Committee

1. "What is it about our church that appeals to you?" is designed to find out whether you have done your homework on their unique context and whether your personal values line up with theirs.
2. "Why do you want to leave your present position?" is designed to find out whether you are running from conflict or are in some other kind of trouble. They also want to know what you have accomplished in terms of God's call to your past church and how you know that God has released you from that situation.
3. "What have you found to be your greatest strengths and weaknesses?" is designed to find out whether you know who you are and whether you are secure enough to express your humanity. They also want to know if any of these weaknesses would be a detriment to the future of their church or whether you have a strategy to minimize them through your other strengths. The key here is to be honest. If you believe that your strengths match the church's needs, then be bold about it. Please, however, don't try to sell yourself if it is clear that these strengths are really not what the church needs at this time.
4. "How would you describe your leadership style?" is designed to find out whether your patterns of leadership will match their expectations. This is the time to give some examples of how you lead and of how you have worked with leaders in your past. There should be no surprises in the future about your leadership style after your candid and detailed discussion of this issue now.
5. "What is your position on _____?" is designed to find out whether your theological and political emphasis is acceptable to the existing church culture and whether you express those positions with graciousness and wisdom. Avoid getting into a lengthy

debate. Be forthright, clear, and simple where you have definite convictions and be honest if you are undecided in any area.

6. "Is there anything else we should know about you?" is designed to elicit information that was not stated in previous profiles or something else that should be touched on. If there is any information that could later be interpreted as your keeping something from the committee, this is the time to raise it and defuse it. For example, if you suffered a forced termination from your previous church, you need to give an honest explanation. This may also be an opportunity to bring up special achievements or qualifications that have not been discussed.

7. "Would you accept this position if it were offered to you?" is designed to find out whether you have a sense of enthusiasm or excitement at the possibility of a ministry partnership together. This is not the time to be academic. Instead, use this opportunity to demonstrate that you have emotions that you are capable of expressing. If you are excited by the prospect of this ministry, then genuinely communicate it while emphasizing that the Holy Spirit must confirm it to you and your spouse when you pray together.[7]

Questions from the Candidate

1. "What do you consider the most pressing needs and concerns that your church is facing both now and in the future?" is designed to find out whether the committee's perceptions have been thoroughly considered. It will also help you to know whether your perceptions and their perceptions closely match.

2. "What would be attractive about this church for a new family in the community, or what might make them not interested?" is designed to discover how the congregation's leaders see themselves. What are they most excited and animated about in their answer? Where do they feel the most sense of ownership and passion? What areas of neglect are they aware of and how strongly do they feel about doing something about it?

3. "What were the previous pastor's greatest strengths? Were there any areas where he could have been stronger?" is designed to discover how balanced the committee members are in their perceptions of leadership. Usually, any estimation that is off the charts in either direction is a sure sign that your future ongoing evaluations will be determined by a hidden or subjective agenda. You are also seeking to discover if there are any areas of pent-up demand based

on a consensus of opinion regarding your predecessor's weaknesses. The next leader will be expected to make up for those deficiencies. Conversely, there may well be an expectation that the new leader will share all of the predecessor's strengths, especially if he was at the helm for more than seven years.

4. "What would be the fastest way for a leader in this church to lose favor with the people?" is designed to discover the specific norms of the church's culture that may not have been evident in the profiles. This question will also reveal some of the specific characteristics of the geographical region that may take precedence over denominational distinctives.

5. "If you could give only one word of advice to a new leader in this church, what would it be?" is designed to discover any "hot buttons" that are unique to this committee or individuals in the group. It may also reveal unresolved conflicts or hurts carried over corporately by the church body, which will affect the new leader.

6. "Why are you interested in me as a serious candidate for this position?" is designed to discover how accurately the committee has perceived the candidate's temperament and gifts. This might be the time to interject a more realistic portrayal of "who you are and who you are not" before moving toward a decision.

After the Interview

A Word from the Search Committee

During the intensive days of looking for God's confirmation on a call, it seems it is always the small things that make a difference. A recent candidate interviewed by our search committee brought along his wife for a weekend stay. They made a reasonably good impression on the members. However, two weeks after the interview, no one had received a thank you note from this couple for the special ways they had been taken care of during the weekend with the church. I watched how this seemingly small oversight began to grow into serious doubts in the minds of two of the more prominent committee members, about whether this front-running candidate would even stay in the race.

Beyond showing common courtesy, a handwritten note of appreciation demonstrates to an overworked and unnoticed search committee that you know the difficult task they face. You also tell them by this action that you are truly interested in them.

A Word from the Candidate

Robert Dingman's research with pastoral candidates revealed these common "pet peeves" from the other side of the table:

1. "Most committees won't spend the money to have their members come and visit you."
2. "When the committee calls a senior pastor for references, he is often less than open, because committees won't keep a confidence."
3. "Very few committees understand what is important to a pastor."
4. "Don't use a seminary professor as a consultant for the search committee. They are usually out of touch."
5. "Some search committees try to be manipulative or are controlled by one person who tries to get his or her candidate in. It becomes a real power struggle."
6. "I get frustrated when search committees do not have a clear understanding of their purpose or task."
7. "When a letter comes to me asking that I fill out a form for them, but it isn't even individually addressed, I toss it. They haven't done their homework and I'm just part of a mass mailing."[8]

According to Dingman, most of his respondents who were seeking a ministry match rated the search committees they encountered as "inept." I hope that most of us will not have to experience what the following pastor went through in a ministry mismatch:

> In the first sixteen years of ministry, my wife and I experienced some incredibly difficult times, which included:
>
> - being placed in a church that didn't want a young pastor and resisted us all the way through our time there
> - being pulled out of a growing church because one person didn't like the growth, a move that devastated both the church and us
> - physical, sexual, and emotional abuse against our family
> - financial hardship in a wealthy church and community, including having to go to the food bank to get enough to eat

- within a half hour after being released from the hospital following a serious car accident, when I was unable even to walk across the room by myself, being confronted by the chairman of the board about people who were upset with my unnecessary time off and who suggested I had better be in the pulpit on Sunday
- hearing our oldest son at age fifteen tell us he was walking away from the church because of all the hypocrites

Then two-and-a-half years ago, we candidated at a small rural church. This time, everything was right. The board sensed God was going to do something great. With the low salary package, we were turned down for a mortgage, but the church felt so strongly that God was in this match, that we were given a twelve-thousand-dollar gift for the down payment and a ten-thousand-dollar interest-free loan! Then God began to move at the church in an unprecedented way. It doubled in size, adding two services and a small group ministry. It has been our dream come true! Even our four children think that our church has lots of "real Christians."

In retrospect, we see that the hardship we experienced prepared us for this ministry. Many times we have been able to embrace a hurting person and say, "We've been there, and with God's help, we'll see you through this difficult time in your life." Our new perspective has shown us the connection between brokenness and ministry. Sometimes, what appears to be a mismatched mistake isn't necessarily the right interpretation. It may be the highway preparation for the coming of the presence of the Lord.

A Word from the Practitioners

Our own research with search committees resulted in this interesting compilation of guidelines reiterated by various groups from different areas:

Ten Don'ts in Staffing a Ministry

1. Don't hire staff with relatives in the church.
2. Don't hire staff who are technically competent, but are not emotionally stable, somehow thinking that you can help "fix" them.

3. Don't hire men or women for your staff who are not "in order" at home, or they will be "out of order" at church.
4. Don't hire a man whose mother was domineering; he will seek to hide things from you as he did with his mother. He will have a tendency to be pathological about telling the truth.
5. Don't hire a couple until you have a feel for their marriage dynamics and are comfortable with them.
6. Don't be deceived by what people boast about; the issues may instead be points of weakness they are seeking to hide.
7. Don't hire anyone who strikes you as immature; they're not ready for ministry responsibilities.
8. Don't delay termination when serious problems resurface; it only gets worse.
9. Don't try to cover for a staff member's shortcomings when they jeopardize the ministry; you will be accused of a credibility shortfall.
10. Don't hire anyone until you or volunteers can no longer do the job yourselves.

Summary

Like a dating relationship moving toward serious discussions of engagement and marriage, the interview cycle is a process that both the church and potential leader must move into prayerfully. Questions of character, competence, and chemistry (connectedness), will be decided in brief but intense interactions. These exhausting and exhilarating times will help to clear or cloud the delicate work of the confirmation process.

While on-site with your spouse, you can enhance and facilitate progress checks with one another between meetings by making brief notes of key thoughts and impressions. These notes will serve you well after you return home, as you discuss the opportunity in more detail and evaluate further developments. They will also be helpful when you ask key mentors for their feedback on your concerns and expectations. Most importantly, these notes will become your testimony of the leading of the Lord as you compare them with the Scriptures God gives you during and after your interview visit.

CHAPTER 11

LEADERSHIP MATCHING FOR THE TWENTY-FIRST CENTURY

A church elder, who served on a pastoral search committee for a mainline church, echoed the thoughts of several laypeople we spoke to regarding the state of church leadership. After spending more than ten months on the committee, reviewing dossiers and interviewing pastoral candidates, he was aghast at what transpired in the search for a new pastor of their 120-year-old church:

> Boy, were my eyes opened. What are the seminaries doing today? We saw candidates, who weren't fit to be a pastor of any church, parade in front of us as if they were the answer to all of mankind's problems. I know there are some very qualified people out there who are doing an outstanding job of leading the church, but I was greatly dismayed at the quality of people we had to choose from. I had held seminaries in higher regard as training grounds for the leaders of the future. Now, I'm very concerned about the future of the church.[1]

Marriages in the New Millennium

Even with all the guidelines and resources we have discussed to help with pastoral and church selection, there are still too many places where both the church and the potential leader can fall into the cracks. Is there any hope for a new model of preparing leaders that can help eliminate many of these problems? Is there a process that will contribute to better matches resulting in better marriages? Is there a new way to confirm the call in the coming millennium? The answer from several quarters is "Yes!" as long as we are willing to go deep enough in dealing with root causes.

I have spoken to numerous alumni who said that their years at seminary were "lost years." Their message was clear: The rigors of academia had not prepared them for the real work of the ministry. Most commonly they reported that the biggest challenge they faced in their congregations was how to create an authentic Christian community and a healthy expression of God's kingdom relationships that would attract the surrounding culture. Tragically, they never experienced this sense of community during their seminary training. For three long years, they sat in rows in classrooms or chapels being taught by professors who themselves were not experiencing community. In addition, they were too busy in their church practicums to do much more than help run programs. Too many of them developed a "performance-based" view of the Christian life, which they carried into their ministry careers. Eventually they grew weary on the treadmill of ministerial busyness.

The sadness in the voices of these eager men and women, who graduated from our finest evangelical schools with inadequate ministry preparation, is painful to hear. The tragedy is compounded by the substantial time, money, and effort they now must spend to cover what was left undone in the academic setting. The litany of data from former students, compiled by George Barna, is sobering:

- Pastors attend an average of three seminars or conferences a year.
- Three-quarters of all senior pastors seek to upgrade their abilities by listening to the teaching tapes of other church leaders or consultants.
- More than nine out of ten senior pastors have read ten Christian books and four non-Christian self-help books in the past year.
- Two-thirds of the pastors view an average of four videotapes a year on ministry techniques.
- Half of all senior pastors said they had hired and interacted with a consultant in the past year.[2]

In addition to these statistics is the startling truth that the majority of seminary graduates who are now pastors are serving small churches, yet more than one-third of the senior pastors leading America's megachurches do not have a seminary degree![3]

In a special study called "The M. J. Murdock Charitable Trust Review of Graduate Theological Education in the Pacific Northwest," director Tim Dearborn concluded his research in these somewhat extreme terms:

> There is no other professional organization in the world which allows its primary professional training institutions to produce graduates who are generally as functionally incompetent as the Church permits its seminaries.[4]

One of the most revealing insights from Dearborn's study is the discrepancy of priorities between those who train pastors and the people who are being led by these pastors. The top five priorities of laymen for their leaders (in order) are:

1. Spirituality
2. Relational skills
3. Character
4. Communication skills
5. Theological knowledge

In contrast, the top five priorities of professors for training pastors are:

1. Theological knowledge
2. Character
3. Leadership
4. Communication skills
5. Counseling skills

From this study, we can see some of the root causes of mismatching in ministry. Church members want spirituality more than any other quality in their leaders, while seminary professors are not even looking for it. The laity see theological knowledge as the lowest priority of the top five, while professors see it as the highest. Relational skills were the second priority from the flock for their shepherds, yet the professors didn't even rate it in the top five. Is it any wonder we are creating situations that require a book like this?

As we step into the new millennium in ministry, we propose five structural solutions to help the body of Christ increase its number of successful, healthy church leadership/ministry partnerships. These will require shifting the standard training paradigms and empowering the pioneers who are willing to explore uncharted territory.

1. Start Ministry Matching Before Ministry Training

We must create new partnerships between churches and our training institutions. This solution begins when a congregation identifies the character and calling of one of its own and commits to invest in his or her life through prayer and mentoring. It continues as the church "sends out" the individual to a school that "receives" him or her and assigns additional mentors who communicate regularly with the home-church mentors. These new mentors could be local church leaders in the immediate area of the school who would also certify the seminary student in skills and character outside of the home church environment. The training process would culminate with the home church placing the graduate on staff or actively fostering a ministry match through its network of contacts.

Carlos, one of our university's outstanding students, was a prototype example of this new training paradigm. Before he enrolled in our program, his home church in New York discipled him and equipped him as an emerging leader. They assigned intercessors and mentors, who confirmed his calling, along with church staff members who had oversight responsibility. His pastor then visited our seminary with Carlos to meet with me and others to discuss our partnership with them in advanced training for Carlos. Once it was determined that he would relocate to our school in Virginia, we entered into phase two of our partnership.

Local church mentors and intercessors were recruited to continue working with Carlos and to communicate with his mentors back in New York. Once every three months, Carlos drove to New York to spend a weekend with his New York mentors and to report to the congregation what he was learning. His Virginia mentors accompanied him on several of these trips and met with his New York mentors. Some of his professors also traveled to New York to minister in his church and meet with the staff to report his progress.

The church invested heavily in this outstanding young man. They continually prayed for him and sent him updates on their ministry development. They sent people to visit him while on business or pleasure trips. They sent money to help him while he worked his way through a joint degree. He was never out of their hearts and minds, even though he was out of state.

A solid delegation of church leaders and members attended Carlos's graduation to celebrate with him. Afterward, they received him back as a full-time staff member in the position for which he had been groomed according to his gifts and values. The church's loyalty and investment in Carlos's personal and academic life has resulted in an outstanding, long-term relationship with him. He remains a staff pastor there after six years. Their partnership with us taught us the value of maintaining relationships with those who know the heart and calling of future leaders. In this critical time for leadership training, we are now asking potential students to seriously consider this model of ministry-matching with their churches, even before their formal training begins.

2. Link Emerging Leaders with School and Church Partnerships During Training and Matching

One of the key reasons for continual mismatches is the way many of our future leaders are being trained. Unfortunately, many of their teachers have migrated to positions as seminary professors as a result of their own pain and disillusionment with mismatched churches. As a seminary professor for twelve years, I have rubbed shoulders with too many colleagues who have a love/hate relationship with the church. Many of these unresolved conflicts come out during lectures in their "off-the-cuff" criticism of churches. Somewhat arrogantly, curriculum, courses, and learning objectives are being designed without the input of those practitioners who are attempting to make ministry relevant to the twenty-first century. It is time for a new partnership between schools and churches to ensure better matches between leaders and ministries!

Following the pattern of training partnerships in the Seattle area described in the Murdock report, educators who design and determine the curriculum for ministry degrees should consult with seasoned practitioners who can feel the pulse of the front line. Specific objectives for each ministry class should include training modules taught by successful leaders who are practicing that discipline or subject in the real world. As much as possible, every ministry class should relocate out of the classroom and into the ministry context itself, including observations and reflections in real-time labs. Students should receive input from seasoned mentors in their ministry setting, mentors who can help evaluate them in hands-on exercises as part of the standard practical ministry courses.

Leith Anderson predicts that most seminaries will have to decide whether to focus on academics or professional training, but they will no longer be able to do both.

> We will need comparatively few graduate schools of theology and comparatively more professional schools of ministry. Both must move away from the traditional notion of education being time and space, but this switch must especially apply to the preparation of practitioners. They want to be men and women who can do something, not know everything.[5]

David Hubbard, president of Fuller Theological Seminary, predicts:

> In the future, we may see one-third to half of education done by people engaged in some form of specialized ministry. We will probably use smaller core faculties and larger adjunct faculties. And we will be farming out more of our education to churches and other Christian agencies. They can be our laboratories.[6]

The prophetic direction of those who are called to train effective leaders is away from the traditional pattern of specialized scholars who spend the majority of their time in classrooms and libraries. The new wineskin is seen in the movement to encourage dual appointments between ministries and schools so that students can learn from teachers who are doing what they teach. What seems to be on the cutting edge today—teachers modeling as well as talking about ministry skills—is simply New Testament leadership principles applied to our day (Acts 1:1; 1 Thess. 2:8).

3. Link Matched Leaders with Area Wide Co-Mentors During the First Year

A 1995 research project at Regent University, involving two hundred pastors, one hundred female ministry leaders, and twenty-seven Christian retreat centers specializing in ministry to leaders, reinforced the necessity of meaningful relationships for longer tenures in ministry. Male pastors identified the following key practices that have enabled them to avoid land mines and to faithfully persevere in the ministry: "develop a close relationship with a mentor" (24%), "maintain peer accountability" (24%), and "surround yourself with men of character for support" (11%). Women in leadership highlighted the importance of "personal support of other women in leadership" (41%). Retreat centers listed "adequate support from mentors and peers" (64%) and "accountability" (28%) as two key elements that wounded leaders are now putting into practice to help them remain faithful, fruitful, and fulfilled. From these data, we acquired a new appreciation for why Jesus sent his disciples out two by two.

In Deuteronomy 24:5, a new husband is told what he can and can't do after taking a new wife. Tough to do today! However, the principle still applies: The first year of a marriage is foundational to its healthy future. In the beginning, the new couple must take extraordinary measures together.

We have seen that the first year of a "ministry marriage" relationship is equally foundational to its healthy future. Over the past decade, a majority of new ministers (65%) began their careers by joining a ministry team rather than starting out as a solo pastor. This new generation of ministers, the "thirty-something" generation, is three times as likely to have prepared for the ministry through an apprenticeship with another minister than is the "fifty-something" generation.[7] The power of co-mentoring, support, encouragement, and accountability relationships is expressed in the way we train and in the way we launch our new leaders into their first years of ministry. The future is here!

When the apostle Paul wrote in 1 Corinthians 4:15, "you do not have many fathers," he could have been painting a prophetic picture of the plight of our modern-day ministers. As they leave school or transition to another church, novice ministers usually move to a new area with no one in sight to provide a mentoring relationship. In the spirit of Malachi 4:6, it is time to "turn the hearts of the fathers to their children" and make the mentoring connection!

Prior to extending or accepting a call, every search committee and candidate should know who from the immediate area will be a mentor or co-mentor to the new leader. Mentors should be drawn from outside the particular church body, and even outside the stream that the church represents. The search committee could recommend several respected "spiritual fathers" in the city, who might serve in this capacity during the critical first year of the ministry match. Perhaps we will see a movement in America soon where the hearts of these "fathers" will be turned toward their spiritual "children" in healthy, supportive, mentoring relationships.

I spent six and a half years leading a church that was a mismatch culturally, socially, geographically, economically, and emotionally. It was difficult for my wife and son to be uprooted from the place where we had been happy in ministry. Today, twelve years later, I can see how God used that season to prepare us for the joy we are now experiencing. Only recently have my wife and I clearly seen that God confirmed our call to that church. The key to our perseverance was the godly mentor we met with once a month during the first year. Without him, we would not have finished well in that church and community. Thank you Dr. Thompson.

4. New Strategies for Churches to Raise Up Their Own Leadership

Peter Wagner has been on the cutting edge of church growth development, prayer movements, and now the "apostolic leadership" patterns in emerging churches around the world. This developing model of church life includes these nine characteristics:

1. New name (nondenominational)
2. New authority structure (return to the apostolic function, minus the requirement to be an "eyewitness")
3. New leadership training (from within the church system rather than sending away to school)
4. New ministry focus (emphasizing New Testament style of church planting)
5. New worship style
6. New prayer forms
7. New finances
8. New outreach
9. New power orientation[8]

While not all churches or church traditions will agree with Wagner's positions, his observations on leadership training have broad application. Recognizing the inadequacy of the present system of marrying "strangers" in traditional ministry/leader matches, Wagner calls for a return to raising up leaders from within our congregations:

> Members of the paid pastoral staff of typical new apos-
> tolic churches are usually homegrown. As all the be-
> lievers in the congregation become active in ministry,
> certain ones tend to rise to the top like cream on fresh
> milk, and they are the ones who are then recruited for
> the staff. Because for many this involves a mid-life ca-
> reer change, the possibility of their enrolling for two or
> three years in the residence program of a typical semi-
> nary or Bible school is extremely remote. . . . Continu-
> ing education for leaders more frequently takes place in
> conferences, seminars and retreats rather than in class-
> rooms of accredited institutions.[9]

At a June 1998 educators' conference for this emerging model, five
advantages of raising up church staff from within the organization were
noted. First, these leaders-in-training already agree with the vision of
the pastor and the values of the church. Second, they have demonstrated
a loyalty to the pastor that has been tried in the fires of conflict. Third,
they are motivated to implement the leaders' vision, because they have
either been led to the Lord by these leaders or have been mentored by
them over the years. Fourth, they know the church and how it operates.
Fifth, they have demonstrated over a period of time that they have the
spiritual gifts for a good ministry match.[10]

5. The Case for "Arranged Marriages"

Around the world and around the block, churches are adopting new
patterns of leadership replacement and succession that have biblical
precedent. Like arranged marriages in Bible times, some African-
American churches pass the leadership mantle within their own families,
while other transitioning pastors proactively recruit replacements from
among those they have know for years—inside or outside the church. A
case can be made that leaders should be publicly and boldly involved in
the selection and installation of those who follow them, just as Elisha
succeeded Elijah (1 Kings 19:16), Solomon succeeded David (1 Chron.
28:5,10), Eleazar succeeded Aaron (Num. 20:24–29), Joshua succeeded
Moses (Exod. 17:9–11; 24:13–14; 32:17), and Timothy succeeded Paul
(Phil. 2:19; Acts 16:1–3; 17:14–15).

Moses personally appointed Joshua (Num. 27:18), set him before the other leaders for them to bear witness and give their support (v. 19), and then set him before the congregation (v. 19). All of these steps involved a public honoring and laying on of hands from the departing leader to the new. Pastor Frank Damazio describes how he followed this biblical pattern when he chose a man from within the ranks to replace him as senior pastor of the church he planted:

> Passing the baton to my successor was exciting. The Lord led us through every step. The elders, my wife, and I laid hands on the new man and his wife and prayed for them. Ahead of time, I had a baton made to give to him. On it, I had a message engraved: *Keep the vision. Run with integrity.* I blessed him and handed the baton to him. I exhorted the elders to run faster and harder in the race. I exhorted the congregation to continue with the vision.
>
> As I handed the baton to my successor, I felt a virtue leave me and enter him supernaturally. In my spirit I saw the mantle lift off my wife and me and rest on him and his wife. I could see the congregation's love transfer to them. In a moment, they were exalted in the eyes of the congregation. The people stood clapping and crying. The people now would follow him as they had followed me. The change was complete. We were free to go and accomplish the will of God for us.[11]

One particular statement, from among the many responses we received during our research of ministry-matching, summarizes the right perspective for all of these detailed deliberations:

> Overall, some of the reasons for the changes along my journey were simply the Lord changing *me* and moving me closer to His ultimate niche for me. I look at each transition as moving closer to His ultimate vision for me, but not to the degree of looking at a position as simply a "step." I think the Lord is concerned about *who* He is making me to be rather than what I happen to be *doing* at the time. Each position, I believe, needs to be

considered not only in terms of what I can offer, but also, what God is going to do in *me* in that place.

This book is dedicated to you, the reader, with the expectation that the grace of God will be greatly upon you in the exciting process of leadership and ministry matching. May He join together what no man can put asunder as He confirms His call in the life of the ministry and the leader.

CONCERT OF PRAYER

Suggested Prayer Concert Format

I recommend starting with a thirty-minute time for food and fellowship, then welcome, announcements, introductions, and overview.

1. Praise in songs
2. Prayers of thanksgiving (short prayers)
3. Testimonies (short illustrations of answered prayers for churches and city)
4. Praise and worship
5. Scriptural declarations (individuals stand to read or quote a relevant passage)
6. Exhortation on repentance (brief Scriptures on the need for brokenness before the Lord)
7. Season of repentance prayers (kneel, come to the altar, etc.)
8. Declaration of cleansing (quote appropriate Scriptures and stand in praise)
9. Devotional teaching (maximum fifteen minutes on some aspect of prayer)
10. Intercessory introduction (three to five minutes explaining the plan for prayers of agreement)
11. Intercessory groups of three (pray for individual needs and churches)
12. Praise (regroup to exalt the Lord)
13. Intercessory groups of seven (pray for crises in our cities, homes, schools, streets, and so on)

14. Praise (regroup to exalt the Lord, testify to what God has just done)
15. Intercessory groups of twelve (pray for city and worldwide evangelism)
16. Victory circle (one large group joining hands to bless those on either side, then all praying at once over the forces of darkness, then the shout of victory and praise)
17. Closing announcements (short reminders while remaining in circle)
18. Fellowship time (finish remaining food and converse in an encouraging, spiritual atmosphere)

Note: This format can be utilized from an hour to a three-hour session. Simply expand or contract various components as the Lord leads.

In a concert of prayer within a single church, individuals can be assigned various Scripture and/or topics of prayer.

In a city-wide concert of prayer with larger numbers, it is appropriate to allow participating church members the freedoms outlined above.

APPENDIX 2

COVENANT FOR A SEARCH COMMITTEE

Recognizing our total dependence on the Lord and pledging to follow the Holy Spirit in the calling of His chosen leader to our church, we agree to serve Him together in the following commitments:

Prayer

- We will pray daily for the Holy Spirit to search our hearts and bring us to continual repentance and purity before our Father.
- We will pray daily for one another that we may be unified in our understanding of the heart and will of our Father.
- We will pray for our church and for the candidates who come before us for confirmation of a call.

Communication

- We will allow one another the freedom to express ideas, feelings, and concerns in an atmosphere of openness.
- We will speak honestly and sincerely with one another without taking offense.
- We will be responsible with privileged information and maintain the confidentially of committee discussions.
- We will preserve the integrity of the committee relationships by not criticizing members or procedures except in face-to-face committee sessions.

Accountability

- We will be both thorough and ethical in all our investigations and evaluations of candidates.
- We will promptly and tactfully notify in writing those candidates dropped from consideration.
- We recognize our accountability to our present church leadership and to our congregation and will communicate regularly and clearly on our progress.
- We will recommend to the church only that candidate whom we can fully support in a spirit of unity.

Signed

_____   _____

_____   _____

_____   _____

CORE VALUES AUDITS

Core Values Audit #1

Directions: Rate each of the core values below from 1 to 5, with 1 being the lowest and 5 the highest.

____   1.   Godly servant leadership
____   2.   A well-mobilized lay ministry
____   3.   Bible-centered preaching and teaching
____   4.   The poor and disenfranchised
____   5.   Creativity and innovation
____   6.   World missions
____   7.   People matter to God
____   8.   An attractive facility
____   9.   Financial responsibility
____   10.   The status quo
____   11.   Welcoming visitors
____   12.   Intercessory prayer
____   13.   Cultural relevance
____   14.   Sustained excellence and quality
____   15.   Fellowship and community
____   16.   Evangelism
____   17.   Strong families
____   18.   A grace-orientation to life
____   19.   Praise and worship
____   20.   A Christian self-image

____ 21. Social justice
____ 22. Committed Christians (discipleship)
____ 23. Tithing and giving
____ 24. Counseling
____ 25. Civil rights and justice concerns
____ 26. Christian education (all ages)
____ 27. The ordinances
____ 28. Racial reconciliation
____ 29. Other:

Write down all the core values—but no more than twelve—that received a rating of 4 or 5. Rank these according to priority by placing the number 1 in front of the highest, 2 in front of the next highest, and so on.

Core Values Audit #2

Directions: The following questions will help you to discover and clarify an established organization's (church or parachurch) core ministry values. Ask people in the organization (leaders, participators, and others) these questions, as well as answering them yourself. Try to answer as many of the questions as possible, even though some of the answers may be similar or identical.

1. Where do you invest your time in this ministry? Why?
2. Where do people invest their money in this organization? Why?
3. What are people inside and outside this ministry saying about it?
4. What is it about this organization that excites you? (What stirs your emotions?)
5. What attracts people like you to this ministry? (Why are you here?)
6. When people brag about this ministry, what specifically do they brag about?
7. What do you and others admire most about this ministry? What do you admire least?
8. If you are a leader in this organization, why are you in a leadership position? What would cause you to resign?
9. If you were a member or an employee of this organization, what would cause you or others to leave?
10. Name one or two changes that would make this a better ministry. What would you not change?
11. If God would grant you one desire for this organization, what would it be?

12. What is most important to this organization? (What is this organization's bottom line?)
13. What are this ministry's core values?
14. What are your ministry core values? Do they agree or disagree with the ministry's core values?

This material was taken from Aubrey Malphurs, *Values Driven Leadership* (Grand Rapids: Baker, 1996), 185–87. Used by permission.

READINESS FOR CHANGE INVENTORY

Directions: Each item below is a key element that will help you to evaluate your church's readiness for change. Strive for objectivity—involve others (including outsiders) in the evaluation process. Circle the number that most accurately rates your church.

1. LEADERSHIP. The pastor and the church board (official leadership) are favorable toward and directly responsible for change. If any influential member (the unofficial leadership, such as the church patriarch or a wealthy member, for example) are also for change, score 5. If moderately so, score 3. If only the secondary level of leaders (other staff, Sunday school teachers, etc.) are for change, while unofficial leadership opposes it, score 1.

5   3   1

2. VISION. The pastor and the board have a single, clear vision of a significant future that looks different from the present. If the pastor is able to mobilize most relevant parties (other staff, boards, and the congregation) for action, score 5. If the pastor, but not the board, envisions a different direction for the church, score 3. If the pastor and board have not thought about a vision, and/or they do not believe that it is important, score 1.

5   3   1

3. VALUES. The church's philosophy of ministry (its core values) includes a preference for innovation and creativity. Though proven forms, methods, and techniques are not discarded at a whim, if the church is more concerned with the effectiveness of its ministries than adherence to traditions, score 5. If moderately so, score 3. If the church's ministry forms and techniques have changed little over the years while its ministry effectiveness has diminished, score 1.

5   3   1

4. MOTIVATION. The pastor and the board have a strong sense of urgency for change that is shared by the congregation. If the congregational culture emphasizes the need for constant improvement, score 3. If the pastor and/or the board (most of whom have been in their positions for many years) along with the congregation are bound by long-standing, change-resistant traditions that discourage risk taking, score 1. If somewhere in between, score 2.

3   2   1

5. ORGANIZATIONAL CONTEXT. How does the change effort affect the other programs in the church (Christian education, worship, missions, and others)? If the individuals in charge are all working together for improvement and innovation, score 3. If some are, score 2. If many are opposed to change or are in conflict with one another over change, score 1.

3   2   1

6. PROCESSES/FUNCTIONS. Major changes in a church almost always require redesigning processes and functions in all the ministries, such as Christian education, church worship, and others. If most in charge of these areas are open to change, score 3. If only some, score 2. If they are turf protectors or if they put their areas of ministry ahead of the church as a whole, score 1.

3   2   1

7. MINISTRY AWARENESS. Does the leadership of your church keep up with what is taking place in the innovative evangelical churches in the community and across America in terms of ministry and outreach effectiveness? Do the leaders objectively compare what the church is doing to that of churches that are very similar? If the

answer is yes, score 3. If the answer is sometimes, score 2. If no, score 1.

3   2   1

8. COMMUNITY FOCUS. Does the church know and understand the people in the community—their needs, hopes, aspirations? Does it stay in direct contact with them? Does it regularly seek to reach them? If the answer is yes, score 3. If moderately so, score 2. If the church is not in touch with its community and focuses primarily on itself, score 1.

3   2   1

9. EVALUATION. Does the church regularly evaluate its ministries? Does it evaluate its ministries in light of its vision and goals? Are these ministries regularly adjusted in response to the evaluation? If all of this takes place, score 3. If some takes place, score 2. If none, score 1.

3   2   1

10. REWARDS. Change is easier if the leaders and those involved in ministry are rewarded in some way for taking risks and looking for new solutions to their ministry problems. Also, rewarding ministry teams is more effective than rewarding solo performances. If this characterizes your church, score 3. If sometimes, score 2. If your church rewards the status quo and a maintenance mentality, score 1.

3   2   1

11. ORGANIZATIONAL STRUCTURE. The best situation is a flexible church where change is well-received and takes place periodically, not every day. If this is true of your church, score 3. If your church is very rigid in its structure and has either changed very little in the last five years or has experienced several futile attempts at change to no avail, score 1. If somewhere in between, score 2.

3   2   1

12. COMMUNICATION. Does your church have a variety of means for two-way communication? Do most understand and use them, and do they reach all levels of the congregation? If so, score 3. If

only moderately true, score 2. If communication is poor, primarily one-way, and from the top down, score 1.

3   2   1

13. ORGANIZATIONAL HIERARCHY. Is your church decentralized (has few if any levels of leadership between the congregation and the pastor or the board)? If so, score 3. If people at the staff level or boards and committees come between the congregation and the pastor or the board, such that more potential exists for them to block essential change, score 1. If somewhere in between, score 2.

3   2   1

14. PRIOR CHANGE. Churches will most readily adapt to change if they have successfully implemented major changes in the recent past. If this is true for your church, score 3. If some change, score 2. If no one can remember the last time the church changed, or if such efforts failed or left people angry and resentful, score 1.

3   2   1

15. MORALE. Do the church staff and volunteers enjoy the church and take responsibility for their ministries? Do they trust the pastor and the board? If so, score 3. If moderately so, score 2. Do few people volunteer and are there signs of low team spirit? Is there mistrust between leaders and followers and between the various ministries? If so, score 1.

3   2   1

16. INNOVATION. The church tries new things. People feel free to implement new ideas on a consistent basis. People have the freedom to make choices and solve problems regarding their ministries. If this describes your church, score 3. If this is somewhat true, score 2. If ministries are ensnared in bureaucratic red tape and permission from on high must be obtained before anything happens, score 1.

3   2   1

17. DECISION MAKING. Does the church leadership listen carefully to a wide variety of suggestions from all members of the congregation? After it has gathered the appropriate information, does it make decisions quickly? If so, score 3. If moderately so, score 2. Does

the leadership only listen to a select few and take forever to make a decision? Is there lots of conflict during the process, and after a decision is made, is there confusion and turmoil? Score 1.

3   2   1

Total Score:

If your score is:

47–57: The chances are good that you may implement change, especially if your scores are high on items 1–3.

28–46: Change may take place but with varying success. Chances increase the higher the score on items 1–3. Note areas with low scores and focus on improvement before attempting change on a large scale.

17–27: Change will not likely take place. Note areas with low scores and attempt to improve them if possible. Consider starting a new church and implementing your ideas in a more change-friendly context.

Used by permission of VISION MINISTRIES INTERNATIONAL. For additional copies @ $3.00 a copy (includes postage and handling), write or call:

Vision Ministries International
5041 Urban Crest
Dallas, TX 75227
214-841-3777

A SELF-EVALUATION OF OUR CHURCH AND MEMBERS

Pastoral Search Committee Survey

Please *do not* sign your name to this survey, but help us by *checking* the appropriate information.

__Male __Female

Age: ___ 16–20 ___ 21–35 ___ 36–49 ___ 50–61 ___ over 62

How long have you been a Christian?

___ 5 years or less ___ 6–10 years ___ over 11 years

Evaluate as follows:

5 = excellent; 4 = good; 3 = fair; 2 = disappointing; 1 = poor

1. How do you rate the church's friendliness to visitors?   5 4 3 2 1

2. How do you rate the church's evangelistic outreach?

5 4 3 2 1

3. How do you rate the church's corporate worship?

5 4 3 2 1

4. How do you rate the church's community life?

5 4 3 2 1

5. How do you rate the ministry of the elders?

5 4 3 2 1

6. How do you rate the biblical content of the sermons?

5 4 3 2 1

7. How do you rate the church's pastoral ministry?

5 4 3 2 1

8. How do you rate the church's counseling ministry?

5 4 3 2 1

9. How do you rate the church's success at mobilizing its available talent?

5 4 3 2 1

10. How do you rate the appeal of this church to your friends, neighbors, and relatives if they were seeking a church home or faith in Christ?

5 4 3 2 1

11. How do you rate the response of visitors whom you have brought to the church? (Answer only if you did so.)

5 4 3 2 1

12. How do you rate the small group ministry?

5 4 3 2 1

13. How do you rate the men's ministry?

5 4 3 2 1

14. How do you rate the women's ministry?

5 4 3 2 1

15. How do you rate your Bible study (if you are in one)?

5 4 3 2 1

16. How would you rate the chances of the homeless or economically disadvantaged being warmly welcomed here?

5 4 3 2 1

17. How would you rate the church's missions interest and commitment?   5 4 3 2 1

18. How would you rate the church's giving to the poor?   5 4 3 2 1

19. How would you rate the church's youth ministry?   5 4 3 2 1

20. How would you rate the Sunday school?   5 4 3 2 1

21. How would you rate the participation of the congregation in being discipled?   5 4 3 2 1

22. How would you rate the appeal of your church to the community at large?   5 4 3 2 1

23. How would you rate the ministry of prayer in the church?   5 4 3 2 1

24. How would you rate your faithfulness in having family or personal devotional times with the Lord?   5 4 3 2 1

25. How would you rate your own activity in sharing your faith in Christ with others?   5 4 3 2 1

26. How would you rate your own activity in building friendships with unbelievers in order to share Christ with them?   5 4 3 2 1

27. How would you rate your own faithfulness in living a consistent Christian life?   5 4 3 2 1

28. How would you rate your own faithfulness in giving at least 10 percent of your income to fund God's work?   5 4 3 2 1

29. How would you rate your own assurance of salvation?   5 4 3 2 1

30. What personal comments or concerns do you
have for the pastoral search committee?   5 4 3 2 1

In your opinion, the three areas of our church that need the most atten-tion right now are:

(Do not list senior pastor. Prioritize by 1,2,3; 1 = high.)

_____ Individual spiritual growth
_____ Serving one another
_____ Outreach/witnessing/evangelism
_____ Prayer
_____ Church unity/more love & fellowship
_____ Discipleship
_____ Personal ministry involvement
_____ Vision for the future
_____ Better communication from leaders
_____ Revival/renewal
_____ Spiritual leadership
_____ Stewardship/tithing/giving
_____ Other (please explain)_____

_____

The spiritual needs in your life not being met by our church are:

How do you feel about the Sunday morning worship service?

Style	*Music*
___ It should be more formal	___ It should be more traditional (hymns)
___ It should be less formal	___ It should be more contempo-rary (choruses)
___ It is about right	___It is about right
___ It should be more traditional	
___ It should be less traditional	

Other comments regarding our worship services: _____
_____

> "In order to reach the unchurched in our community
> and meet their needs, I would be willing to support major
> changes in the church as long as we held to God's truth."

What are your responses to this statement?

Thank you for your consistent prayers and support. Please note any prayer requests you may have:

For the Search Committee's Evaluation

1. What did you learn from this self-evaluation survey of your church and its members?

2. Are there specific items addressing your present situation?

3. Decide if you wish to use this in your process.

After you have completed your survey of the congregation, you are ready for the next step.

Identifying Your Church Profile

1. What are the church's core values?

2. What is your church's history?

3. Write a brief summary of the origin and development of your church's ministry.

4. Summarize factors affecting the growth or decline of the church.

5. Provide a general description of the ministry style of former pastors and their length of service.

6. What is your membership, past and present?

7. What does the church look like?

8. What is your average church worship attendance?

9. What is the average attendance of your Sunday school, small group ministries, and other ministries?

10. What are the attendance trends over the last decade?

11. Demographic composition—What kind of people attend the church?

12. Evaluation of current ministries emphasis—What is the church focusing on?

13. Congregational involvement—What percentage of people are involved in ministry?

14. Strengths and weaknesses—How well are they doing ministry?

15. Describe your facilities and properties.

- Seating capacity of the worship center?
- Date built?
- Condition of lighting, sound, and interior decorating?
- Is your educational space adequate?
- Do you have fellowship facilities and seating for major church events?
- Administrative facilities: Is your office space adequate?
- Parking: How many spaces do you have? Are they adequate for growth?
- Church location: Describe its setting.
- Property limitations and possibilities for future expansion?
- Present situation and challenges in your facilities?

16. Describe the church's preferred worship style:

The major portion of these materials were taken from Dennis Baker, *A Manual for Pastoral Search Committees of the Conservative Baptist Association of Southern California* (D.Min. Dissertation, Talbot School of Theology, Biola University, 1992).

SAMPLE REFERENCE CHECK FORM

Note: This is a confidential form that will only be used by our search committee during the process of seeking a candidate for a position. It will be destroyed after our search process is completed and will not be used for any other purpose.

Candidate's Name: _____

1. What is your relationship to the candidate and how long have you known each other?

2. What do you consider the candidate's greatest strengths and ministry skills?

3. In what areas do you think the candidate most needs to improve?

4. What do other leaders think of the candidate's character and ministry?

5. What do the people in the candidate's church or ministry think of his/her character and ministry? Is this a divided opinion or a widely held opinion?

6. Is there anything negative about his/her personal life that could harm the candidate's next ministry?

7. Is the candidate's marriage and family life strong and healthy?

8. Briefly describe this person's leadership style.

9. Would you want him/her as your leader? Why or why not?

10. What has not been asked here that might be important for us to know as we consider him/her as our next leader?

References

Please supply seven references. Each should be able to assess the way you function in ministry, your ministry style (model), and your spiritual giftedness. List full addresses, phone numbers, and a brief description of your relationship. These references will be contacted. Do not list any references to whom you are related to by marriage or birth. Indicate by an asterisk (*) those from your current church. Indicate by a check in the box preceding the name if you must be reached personally before the church contacts these references. There should be at least one woman within the list of references. They should include:

- At least one, no more than two, pastors who know you and your work
- An active elder/leader in your current (or most recent) church
- Two additional lay persons in your current (or most recent) church
- A business person who knows you well
- No more than one seminary professor

Note: All pastoral search committees will ask for references from additional persons to contact about you and your ministry.

Name _____

Home phone _____

Home address _____

Office phone _____

City _____

State _____ Zip _____

Relationship to you _____

Name _____

Home phone _____

Home address _____

Office phone _____

City _____

State _____ Zip _____

Relationship to you _____

Name _____

Home phone _____

Home address _____

Office phone _____

City _____

State _____ Zip _____

Relationship to you _____

Name _____

Home phone _____

Home address _____

Office phone _____

City _____

State _____ Zip _____

Relationship to you _____

INDIVIDUAL LEADERSHIP DEVELOPMENTAL TIME LINE

Using J. Robert Clinton's text, *The Making of a Leader,* do the following assignments to enable you to describe your individual "Leadership Developmental Time Line."

1. Answer questions 1, 2, and 3 on page 55.

2. Answer questions 3, 4, 5, and 6 on page 75.

3. Answer questions 1, 2, 3, 4, and 5 on pages 96–97.

4. Answer questions 2 and 3 on page 124.

5. Answer questions 1 and 3 on pages 149–50.

6. Answer question 1 on page 173 briefly.

7. Answer questions 1 and 2 on page 194 briefly.

CALLING THE RIGHT SENIOR PASTOR

(Screening Out the Wrong Ones) A Step-by-Step Process

Senior Pastor Potential Candidate List

When the résumés and names start to come in, this list will be your "best friend."

Senior Pastor Search Questions

(As a committee, customize this form emphasizing the questions that you believe are "must know" and adding any others.)

Briefly describe in short phrases on a separate sheet of paper answers to the following:

Core Values
1. What are the three to five core values that give you the greatest passion in ministry?
2. What should be the core values of the church you would want to pastor?
3. Describe the content of a worship service that fulfills your core values.

Ministry Preferences

1. What do you see as the role of music in worship, and what range of styles do you think are appropriate?
2. What are your views on church growth and planting? (for example, becoming a megachurch or spawning several smaller churches)
3. What criteria do you tend to use to evaluate success in ministry?
4. In outreach and missions, what is the correct balance between meeting physical and spiritual needs?
5. What do you feel should be the balance of the church's involvement in local/cross-cultural outreach?
6. What approaches to evangelism do you feel are most effective? What are you doing presently to cultivate relationships with non-believers?
7. What is your favorite Bible translation? Why?
8. How often do you think a church should celebrate a communion service? What is your preferred method?
9. On what social and moral issues do you feel the church should take a stand? How is this properly expressed?
10. Is your teaching style more topical, expository, or narrative? What do you feel the correct balance is between these?
11. What balance do you strike between application and instruction in a sermon?
12. In what ways can leaders best communicate their vision for the church?
13. What is the place of the small group in the life of the church? What is the ideal structure and content of a small group?
14. What is the church's responsibility in family traumas, such as child and wife abuse, abortion, homosexuality, sexual immorality, substance abuse, and chronic unemployment?
15. What emphasis should the church have with youth and children?

Doctrine

1. What is your view of the church government (elders, line of authority, congregational government, and so on)?
2. How do you view the role of elder(s) in the church? Describe the relationship between the senior pastor and the elders. What scriptural passages support this view?
3. How do you view the role of deacon(s) in the church?
4. Do you or have you worked with deaconesses? Your views?

5. What are your views on a woman in ministry leadership positions in the church?
6. What do you believe and practice in charismatic gifts such as tongues, interpretation of tongues, prophecy, and so on?
7. What do you believe and practice regarding the ministry of healing?
8. How do you relate to those within your church with a different view of spiritual gifts?
9. What is your view on the "spiritual warfare" movement?
10. What are your views on demonic activity in the lives of believers and nonbelievers? What should the church do to minister to these needs?
11. What is the significance of the virgin birth?
12. Was Christ's death on the cross absolutely necessary? Why or why not?
13. What does Christ's resurrection mean for us?
14. How does a person become a Christian?
15. What are the motives for church discipline?
16. Give your understanding of the inspiration, authority, and inerrancy of the Scriptures.
17. Give a biblical view of baptism and explain its purpose.

Personal
1. What do you feel are your spiritual gifts? How have they been affirmed and confirmed?
2. What are your personal strengths? Weaknesses?
3. What do you like most about the ministry? Least?
4. How would you describe your temperament? Your social style? How do you use this "style" to build teamwork?
5. How have you handled bouts of anger, depression, and anxiety?
6. If there has been a time when you were hurt deeply, please describe. What did you learn from this experience?
7. Describe your personal prayer and devotional life.
8. How do you organize and prioritize your week's work, study, sermon preparation, counseling, visitation, devotions, days off, physical fitness, and so on?
9. Name some Christian leaders or thinkers, past or present, who have had the most influence on your ministry life.
10. What sports, hobbies, or spare-time activities do you participate in regularly? Which of these activities include your family?

12. Which magazines do you read regularly?
13. What are your favorite TV programs? How many hours a week do you work on a computer?
14. Give the titles and authors of three Christian and three non-Christian books you have read most recently.
15. What books have influenced your views on leadership?
16. Have you ever left a ministry position due to problems? If yes, please explain.
17. Referring to the Church Profile, do you feel God has prepared you with a vision and gifts for this work?
18. If you were to move to our area, would it create too great a separation from your extended family?
19. What is the order of your priorities regarding your responsibilities to the church and your responsibilities to your wife and children?
20. Describe the "quality" time spent with your family and your family devotional life.
21. How has your wife influenced you in your personal and spiritual growth?
22. How do your wife's gifts complement your marriage?
23. What ministries is your wife currently involved with?
24. What geographical area do you consider to be your home? What geographical area does your wife consider to be home?
25. What are your personal, professional, and family goals over the next ten years?
26. What steps are you taking to achieve these goals?
27. What have been the greatest hindrances you have faced in reaching your goals?
28. What is your personal practice in regard to tithing? What is your view of tithes and offerings in the local church?
29. How would you evaluate your interpersonal skills?
30. What results have you seen in ministry in the last three years?
31. Have you ever led a church through a building program?

Evaluating Your Potential Candidate

With these materials, conversations, and reference checks, you will be able to develop a pretty good profile on a candidate. Does this profile fit your church profile? Only after doing this foundational work should preaching ability be examined.

Poor preaching will subject the pastor to the kind of criticism that can discourage an otherwise good leader. It is best to hear the potential candidate preach on his own "turf" to truly sense if he is connecting with his congregation on a regular basis.

Reviewing the Basics

You now have to make a decision. Is this the man that God wants you to invite to candidate at your church? Return to the basics and ask yourself questions like:

- Has he agreed to candidate if invited?
- Is he excited and challenged by your ministry opportunity? How do you know?
- Is he the right "fit"?
- Have we told ourselves the truth?
- Has the sovereign hand of God been evident in the "process"?
- Are we trying to talk ourselves into this particular person?
- Have we adequately clarified and identified his expectations of us?
- Have we adequately clarified and identified our expectations of him?
- Are these realistic?
- Do his social style and leadership gift match our church at this stage of its history?
- Is he a producer? (Has he fostered growth in his former positions; has the growth remained?)
- Is he still a learner? Is he teachable?
- Is he likable? Respectable? Dependable? Authentic? Believable?
- How is his work ethic?
- Is he balanced enough?
- Is he a healthy person?
- Have we read his heart correctly?
- Are we comfortable with his wife and home life?
- Are we "sold"? Is this an exclamation mark (!) or a question mark (?)?
- In the spirit of Luke 2:52, is he a "compelling person"?
- Is his mission our mission? If yes, then
- Are his operating principles our operating principles? If yes, then
- Are his techniques and approaches our techniques and approaches? If yes, then
- Does his personality match our personality? If yes, then
- Are his problems and challenges our problems and challenges?

Examining the Decision

Once again consult the Lord in prayer. Then return to the following questions as honestly and objectively as possible:

- Have you defined the situation accurately?
- Have you looked at your ministry from the potential candidate's point of view?
- Are you ready to trust this man as your pastor and give him your loyalty?
- Do you need more time to discuss and pray through the decision?
- Are you confident that your decision will be as right over a long period of time as it seems now?
- Do you have any nagging doubts or qualms about this decision?

Now you are ready to come to a consensus on your candidate!

Presenting the Final Choice

Your next move is to phone the candidate and inform him of your decision. Assuming he says yes, *remember to be ethical*. You are still dealing with a person who may be serving in another place of ministry. Therefore, don't fax the information around the country to all your prayer partners and Christian friends — yet.

Your second step is the final composition of the official letter inviting him to candidate. Also, maintain very close communication with your candidate at this stage of the process. Inform him of each step you take. The following very workable strategy is suggested:

Develop a packet from the pastoral search committee that presents the candidate to the church family.
- Inform them of the rationale for your choice.
- Write a summary page of your church's needs to attach to this letter.
- Include your Position Description and Pastoral Profile. (A summary of the search process is very instructive for the congregation.)
- Send a brief biography with a picture of the family and some appropriate comments to share with the entire church. These can be gleaned from your extensive reference file.
- Attach a schedule of the candidating experience.

Arrange to have a church business meeting following the candidating period for the purpose of voting on or confirming the calling of the pastor in accordance with the guidelines of your church constitution and bylaws.

These materials were adapted from Dennis Baker's unpublished D.Min. project from Talbot School of Theology, 1992.

MINISTRY
SELF-EVALUATION FORMS

1. How did God confirm your call to the ministry? Have you ever deeply doubted this call?

2. The role of vision in ministry leadership is of the highest priority. Briefly describe your ministry vision. How do you best communicate that vision to the congregation?

3. Most people resist change initially. How do you prepare your congregation for change and help them during the process of making changes?

4. How does your personal spirituality relate to your work in the ministry?

5. How do you facilitate the expression of unity among church leaders and congregation members?

6. Jesus took His disciples to a deserted place to rest after a period of intense ministry. How do you experience "rest" in the Lord, and what value is it to your ministry?

7. What concerns do you have about opening yourself up to others in the leadership team or in the congregation? How does this affect the way you tend to share responsibility and authority in your ministry?

Self-Perception/Evaluation

Essential Functions of Ministry

There is general agreement that the following functions are essential to pastoral effectiveness. Using the five-point scale that follows, rate yourself for each of the functions by circling the appropriate number.

5. Very effective (top 5%)
4. Quite effective (significant achievement)
3. Effective (more effective than ineffective)
2. Somewhat effective (some instances of achievement)
1. Minimal effectiveness (limited competence or achievement)

1. *Preaching:* Preparing and delivering of clear and convincing sermons that help hearers grow in the knowledge of God and apply His word to their daily lives.   5 4 3 2 1

2. *Worship:* Planning and designing worship experiences that lead the congregation to express praise, gratitude, devotion, and service to God.   5 4 3 2 1

3. *Teaching:* Understanding the learning process and using creative methods to teach in the way people learn.   5 4 3 2 1

4. *Evangelism:* Communicating God's good news about Christ Jesus in the power of the Holy Spirit, in ways that are relevant to the hearers,

with the intent that people embrace Him as their
Savior and Lord.   5 4 3 2 1

5. *Pastoral Care:* Exhibiting a "shepherd's heart,"
   showing by word, action, and presence an understanding of people and their needs, and providing assistance when appropriate and feasible.   5 4 3 2 1

6. *Visitation:* Being among the people, members and
   nonmembers alike, in their homes and work set-
   tings, to develop relationships and meet needs.   5 4 3 2 1

7. *Equipping:* Encouraging, training, and mobilizing people in the discovery and use of their gifts
   and talents for ministry in the context of daily
   living and the church.   5 4 3 2 1

8. *Leadership Development:* Recognizing leadership potential in others and providing opportunities for developing those leadership skills.   5 4 3 2 1

9. *Counseling:* Providing constructive help personally or by directing those in need to specialized,
   trained professionals or other care-givers.   5 4 3 2 1

10. *Administration:* Managing the church's day-to-
    day operations as well as the human and finan-
    cial resources.   5 4 3 2 1

11. *Vision Casting:* Communicating a vision of what
    the people or congregation can achieve, and then
    setting goals accordingly.   5 4 3 2 1

12. *Planning:* Establishing strategies and action
    plans to accomplish agreed-upon goals.   5 4 3 2 1

13. *Motivating:* Sharing dreams, goals, and plans
    in such a way that people want to be personally
    involved.   5 4 3 2 1

14. *Evaluating:* Engaging in the process of comparing what is with what ought to be, for the purpose of determining direction for ministry or areas for improvement.   5 4 3 2 1

15. *Conflict Management:* Managing or resolving opposition occurring as a result of differing viewpoints.   5 4 3 2 1

Models of Ministry

Studies have shown that pastors, by practice, fit into certain ministry models. Their preferred and predominant approach to ministry is expressed in discernible ways. Look over the following nine models and indicate the *one* that best describes your *primary* approach to ministry. Then, note your *secondary* approach to ministry.

Pastor-Shepherd

The minister spends the majority of his time visiting in homes and hospitals. He is known as a pastor who cares. Counseling has a high priority, as well as positive interpersonal relationships.

1. Believes ministry is primarily developing right relationships with God and with other people.
2. Purpose in preaching is to help people develop and mature as individuals so that their relationships can become increasingly more satisfying.
3. To some degree, could be compared to a counselor in the secular world.

Preacher-Teacher

This is an educational model. This person understands his role primarily as a teacher of the truths of Scripture, helping people to apply them to contemporary life. This person is more satisfied in the pulpit and the study than anywhere else.

1. Believes ministry is primarily serving God by being a "servant of the Word" who teaches correct biblical truth.
2. Purpose in preaching is to impart correct biblical knowledge that will provide Christians with the resources they need to live in

obedience to God's Word. Sermons are generally expositions of extended passages of Scripture.

3. To some degree, could be compared to a teacher in the secular world.

Worship Leader

This minister's primary concern is with personal and corporate worship. He finds great satisfaction in planning meaningful services and leading his congregation to experience the awesome holiness of God in worship.

1. Believes ministry is primarily leading the congregation in worship that is pleasing to God.
2. Purpose in preaching is to enrich the congregation's experience of God in worship, so sermons often deal with the nature and actions of God.
3. To some degree, could be compared to a director of drama in the secular world.

Evangelist

The primary concern for this person is to win the lost to Christ and assimilate them into the church. He may do this through personal visitation and his pulpit ministry. He will be very concerned about the numerical growth of the church. He will also have a high degree of interest in missions.

1. Believes ministry is primarily winning people to Christ and building His church.
2. Purpose in preaching is to motivate people to make decisions for Christ and join the church; sermons, therefore, are generally evangelistic.
3. To some degree, could be compared to a salesman in the secular world.

Equipper

This model of ministry has a high commitment to the ministry of the laity. This person often sees himself as a coach and the church members as players on the team. He will derive satisfaction more from the accomplishments of people he has trained than from "hands on" ministry of his own.

1. Believes ministry is primarily helping people develop their spiritual gifts so they can engage in ministry themselves.

2. Purpose in preaching is to recruit and develop Christians for ministry. Sermons generally deal with the nature and ministry of the church.
3. To some degree, could be compared to a player-coach in the secular world.

Church Manager

The pastor sees himself as similar to a corporate executive. He man-
ages the resources of the congregation well. The life of the congregation
is carefully organized and lines of authority are well defined.

1. Believes ministry is primarily managing the varied resources of the
   church with effectiveness and efficiency.
2. Purpose in preaching is to build the church of Christ. Sermons generally deal with the nature and structure of the church.
3. To some degree, could be compared to a corporate executive in the
   secular world.

Prophet

This person will be concerned to challenge the unrighteousness he
perceives in society. Righteousness and justice will be dominant themes
in his ministry. Sermons will compare the contemporary social scene
with prophetic biblical truth.

1. Believes ministry is primarily confronting individuals and institutions with the demands of God's Word for justice, mercy, and
   holiness.
2. Purpose in preaching is to expose personal and corporate injustice
   and unrighteousness with the light of biblical truth.
3. To some degree, could be compared to a social worker/activist in
   the secular world.

Spiritual Director

This minister sees his major role as providing an example for the
congregation. His life is a model, not only of what the Christian life is
like, but also of how it can best be lived. He is the guide church members
use in developing their Christian lives.

1. Believes ministry is setting an example of a simple life of holiness
   and devotion.

2. Purpose in preaching is to help Christians develop a more meaningful relationship with Christ. Sermons often deal with the personal and devotional aspects of life.

3. This model does not compare to any secular occupation, since this person sees ministry as a unique spiritual service.

General Practitioner

This minister is a combination of the other models. His image will be in flux as he changes to meet what he perceives to be the varying needs of the congregation. The members of his church will not share any single image of his work.

1. Believes ministry is meeting the needs of individuals, groups, or the church by using appropriate skills and abilities that he has developed.

2. Purpose in preaching is to help meet congregational needs that are perceived as most acute at that time. Sermons may vary in style and content as the need indicates.

3. To some degree, could be compared to a general practitioner in medicine.

Based on this brief overview of models of ministry, I would say

• My primary approach to ministry is:

• My secondary approach is:

These materials were adapted from Dennis Baker's unpublished D.Min. project from Talbot School of Theology, 1992.

SEEING YOUR CHURCH FROM THE CANDIDATE'S POINT OF VIEW

As you continue preparing for your personal interviews, take some time to think through your process and the opportunity you present from the candidate's point of view.

Every candidate will come into your ministry setting with a different viewpoint and a unique way of seeing things in your church. As he looks around, he will be learning what makes you "tick." For instance, he may scope out the following:

1. Do the people carry and use their Bibles during the service?
2. Was there a sense of joy and expectation during worship, ministry, prayer, and preaching?
3. What is the gender, ethnic, and generational makeup of the church?
4. What evidence of ministry impact is there in the community?
5. Does the church family appear to be unified?
6. Was the previous pastor held in high esteem? Why and how did he leave?
7. Can I be myself here? Is this a place where I can continue to grow as a Christian and in the use of my ministry gifts?
8. Will I be allowed the luxury and freedom to be innovative, even if occasionally I fail?

9. Is this a sufficient challenge with adequate potential for God-glorifying growth.
10. Do I sense a growing desire to be in this place because it is the will and direction of God?
11. What is the depth and width of the church's prayer ministry?
12. Are these people, with their cultural and educational backgrounds, my kind of people?
13. Was the general atmosphere and climate of the church conducive to the praise and worship of God?
14. Does the actual attendance I saw match the figures I was told?
15. What is the quality of the church staff? Do they have a commitment to excellence?
16. Was an attitude of warmth and friendliness conveyed by church staff and leaders?
17. Were the greeters sensitive and helpful?
18. Is this church "user friendly" to the unchurched? Can newcomers find their way around?
19. Is this church accessible to the physically handicapped?
20. Were guests made to feel comfortable or were they embarrassed?
21. Would I bring my friends to this church if I weren't the pastor?
22. Was the worship team adequately prepared and culturally relevant?
23. Is this church introverted or extroverted?
24. What do the cars look like in the parking lot? Does that match the neighborhood?

As the potential candidate interacts with the pastoral search committee, the elder board, church leaders, and staff (if any), he will be asking pointed questions. Many of these will be based on the Church Profile and other materials you have provided him with. For instance:

1. What is the true vision and purpose of this ministry?
2. Is the church organized, programmed, and staffed toward that end?
3. Does the budget of the church reflect the stated ministry priorities?
4. Is the church financially healthy? What is the debt load?
5. Is there a need for building/remodeling in the near future?
6. Does the church exhibit any abnormalities or idiosyncrasies that impede productive, effective, God-honoring ministry?
7. Is the Board reliable and respectable?
8. Does the pastor have to attend all of the meetings of the church?

9. Do the church leaders show evidence of a warm, contagious faith in the Lord Jesus Christ?
10. Are there any skeletons in the closet of the church? If so—what are they, and what was done?
11. Do church leaders practice tithing/generous giving to the church?
12. Are people uptight about who is compensated monetarily for ministry skills?
13. What day(s) of the week did the last pastor take off?
14. Does the church have in print a policy manual of standard operating procedures?
15. How does this church cooperate with other local churches?

LEADERSHIP DEVELOPMENT EVALUATION QUESTIONS

1. What gifts and strengths has the individual shown over the past six months or year? What has he or she done well?

2. Has the individual fulfilled the requirements or guidelines of his or her present role over the past six months or year?

3. Have individuals within the church given positive or negative feedback concerning this person's leadership, ministry, character, relationships, and attitudes? Give appropriate details.

4. What areas has this person shown over the past six months or year that need further development?

5. How do other leaders evaluate the strengths or weaknesses of this person?

6. As a result of this evaluation, should there be any changes made in job descriptions or accountability procedures?

ENDNOTES

Introduction

1. Under the supervision of the author, a fifteen-member team of graduate students from Regent University School of Divinity during 1997 and 1998 conducted a mail-in survey of 120 pastors from evangelical and charismatic/Pentecostal churches, 350 alumni of fifteen Bible schools and seminaries, and ten denominational leaders. Much of the material for this book was drawn from these surveys, as well as from follow-up phone calls made to 5 percent of the survey sample. As the designer and coordinator of the yearlong internship ministry, the author has matched hundreds of emerging leaders with churches, many of whom have gone on to full-time staff positions. In his twenty-four years of ministry, he has served as an executive pastor to a fourteen-hundred-member church, twice as a senior pastor to congregations ranging from two hundred to five hundred members, and three times as an associate pastor. Most recently, he has overseen the planting of several churches and has trained pastors and missionaries from more than thirty denominations at the seminary level.

Chapter 1

1. Andre Bustanoby, "Why Pastors Drop Out," *Christianity Today*, 7 January 1977.
2. George Barna, *Today's Pastors* (Ventura, Calif.: Regal, 1993), 52.
3. John C. LaRue Jr., "Forced Exits: High Risk Churches," *Your Church*, May–June 1996, 72.
4. For further information on the Pastor in Residence ministry, contact Dr. Chuck Wickman or the author at 757-495-7889 or 757-226-4419.
5. John C. LaRue Jr., "Forced Exits: Personal Effects," *Your Church*, November–December 1996, 64.

6. See chapter 3 in Gordon MacDonald's *Ordering Your Private World* for an excellent discussion of being "driven" or being "called" (Nashville: Oliver-Nelson, 1985).
7. Kenneth Alan Moe, *The Pastor's Survival Manual* (Bethesda, Md.: Alban Institute, 1995), vi. For a description of specific behaviors associated with addiction observed by this author, see page 60ff.
8. Louis McBurney, *Every Pastor Needs a Pastor* (Waco, Tex.: Word, 1977).

Chapter 2
1. Gary Smalley and John Trent, in their landmark book *The Blessing*, bring out the implications of the biblical blessing narratives for today's families and church members (Nashville: Nelson, 1986).
2. Robert Dingman, *In Search of a Leader: The Complete Search Committee Guide Book* (Westlake Village, Calif.: Lakeside, 1994), 30.
3. Neil Anderson and Miles Mylander, *Setting Your Church Free* (Ventura, Calif.: Regal, 1995). Many pastors taught by the author have used the principles of this book, and the stories of release for churches are very encouraging.
4. George Barna, *Leaders on Leadership* (Ventura, Calif.: Regal, 1997), 298.
5. See the C. Peter Wagner book series, especially *Churches That Pray* (Ventura, Calif.: Regal, 1993).
6. See Ted Haggard's excellent book *Primary Purpose* for a discussion of how to raise the water level of the Holy Spirit in your community by helping numbers of churches prosper (Orlando, Fla.: Creation House, 1995).

Chapter 3
1. Leith Anderson, "Search Committees: A Strategy for Success," *Christianity Today,* 18 April 1980, 34.

Chapter 4
1. Jack Hayford, *Pastors of Promise* (Ventura, Calif.: Regal, 1997), 145.
2. Aubrey Malphurs, *Values Driven Leadership* (Grand Rapids: Baker, 1996), 13ff.

Chapter 5
1. Lyle Schaller, *Create Your Own Future!* (Nashville: Broadman, 1991), 31.

2. Aubrey Malphurs, *Vision America: A Strategy for Reaching a Nation* (Grand Rapids: Baker, 1994), 175ff.
3. Tommy Teague, *The Revitalization of the Downtown Church* (D.Min. dissertation, Regent University Divinity School, 1998), 37ff.
4. Henry A. Virkler, *Choosing a New Pastor* (Nashville: Oliver Nelson, 1992), 36.

Chapter 6
1. George Mallone, "Picking the Right People" (unpublished teaching notes, 1980).
2. Jack Hayford, *Pastors of Promise* (Ventura, Calif.: Regal, 1997), 139ff.
3. C. Peter Wagner, *Prayer Shield* (Ventura, Calif.: Regal, 1992), 79.
4. Robert Dingman, *In Search of a Leader: The Complete Search Committee Guidebook* (Westlake Village, Calif.: Lakeside, 1994), 154.
5. Ibid., 161–62.

Chapter 7
1. From "First-Class Christians, Second-Class Citizens," by Larry Burkett, reprinted by Biblical Wellness Ministries, Raleigh, N.C., November 1996 newsletter.
2. J. Robert Clinton, *The Making of a Leader* (Colorado Springs: NavPress, 1988).
3. Gary Smalley and John Trent, *The Blessing* (Nashville: Nelson, 1986).

Chapter 8
1. Christopher C. Moore, *Opening the Clergy Parachute* (Nashville: Abingdon, 1995), 86.
2. David B. Biebel and Howard W. Lawrence, eds., *Pastors Are People Too* (Ventura, Calif.: Regal, 1986), 62.
3. Loren Mead, *Your Next Pastorate* (Bethesda, Md.: Alban Institute, 1993), 72.
4. Ibid., 71–74.

Chapter 9
1. Henry T. Blackaby and Henry Brandt, *The Power of the Call* (Nashville: Broadman, 1997), 17–18.
2. See appendix 9 for "Ministry Self-Evaluation Forms."

3. David Keirsey and Marilyn Bates, *Please Understand Me: Character and Temperament Types* (Del Mar: Prometheus Nemesis, 1978). Chapter one includes this instrument.
4. Bob Biehl, Masterplanning Group International, P.O. Box 952499, Lake Mary, FL 32795. For Masterplanning catalog, call 1-800-443-1976.
5. University Associates International, Ltd., Challenge House, 45–47, Victoria Street, Mansfield, Notts. NG18 5 SU, England.
6. James M. Kouzes and Barry Z. Posner, *Leadership Practices Inventory (LPI),* 2d ed. (San Francisco: Jossey-Bass Pfeiffer, 1997). Can be ordered by calling 1-800-569-0443, or on the Internet at: http://www.pfeiffer.com
7. Ibid., 4.
8. Charles E. Fuller Institute of Evangelism and Church Growth, P.O. Box 91990, Pasadena, CA 91109-1990, 1-800-999-9578. Currently available through the International Center for Leadership Development and Evangelism at 1-800-804-0777.
9. Mels Carbonell, *Discover Your Giftedness,* 1996, Uniquely You, P.O. Box 490, Blue Ridge, GA 30513. Can be ordered by calling 1-800-501-0490.
10. Aubrey Malphurs, *Pouring New Wine Into Old Wineskins* (Grand Rapids: Baker, 1993).
11. Terry Nance, *God's Armor Bearer* (Tulsa, Okla.: Harrison House, 1990).

Chapter 10
1. Dennis Baker, D.Min. Dissertation, Talbot School of Theology, 1992, 6–17.
2. The Pastor-in-Residence (P.I.R.) Ministry gives former leaders a "platform" from which to candidate since they are now considered a staff person in the P.I.R. church.
3. Christopher C. Moore, *Opening the Clergy Parachute* (Nashville: Abingdon, 1995), 43.
4. Numerous research studies in business schools continue to support the view that the selection interview contributes little to the prediction of successful work performance.
5. Rev. William Leach, Assemblies of God Michigan District Superintendent, recommends that the candidate's family spend a week at the church and that the candidate preach on two Sundays.
6. Roy Oswald, *New Beginnings: A Pastorate Start Up Workbook* (Bethesda, Md.: Alban Institute, 1993), 31.
7. Moore, *Opening the Clergy Parachute,* 93ff. See appendix 10 for questions to help in the matching process.

8. Robert Dingman, *In Search of a Leader: The Complete Search Committee Guidebook* (Westlake Village, Calif.: Lakeside, 1994), 139ff.

Chapter 11

1. George Barna, *Today's Pastors* (Ventura, Calif.: Regal, 1993), 139–40.
2. Ibid., 144.
3. Leith Anderson, *A Church for the Twenty-First Century* (Minneapolis: Bethany House, 1992), 27.
4. Tim Dearborn, "Preparing Leaders for the Future . . . Today!" Seattle Association for Theological Education, July 1995.
5. Anderson, *Church for the Twenty-First Century,* 47.
6. George Brushaber, "The Twenty-First Century Seminary," *Christianity Today,* 17 May 1993, 46.
7. John C. LaRue Jr., "Forced Exit Survival Guide," *Your Church,* July–August 1996, 64.
8. These are described in his book, *The New Apostolic Churches: Rediscovering the New Testament Model of Leadership and Why It Is God's Desire for the Church Today* (Ventura, Calif.: Regal, 1998).
9. Ibid., 20–21.
10. See appendix 11.
11. Frank Damazio, *The Vanguard Leader* (Portland, Ore.: Bible Temple, 1994), 290–91.